THE BLACKROOM EXPERIENCE

THE BLACKROOM EXPERIENCE

"Keys to Building A Seamless, yet NOT Flawless Mother-Daughter Relationship"

Lisa Thorpe-Vaughn

XULON PRESS

Xulon Press Elite
2301 Lucien Way #415
Maitland, FL 32751
407.339.4217
www.xulonpress.com

© 2017 by Lisa Thorpe-Vaughn

All rights reserved solely by the author. The author guarantees all contents are original and do not infringe upon the legal rights of any other person or work. No part of this book may be reproduced in any form without the permission of the author. The views expressed in this book are not necessarily those of the publisher.

Unless otherwise indicated, Scripture quotations taken from the King James Version (KJV) – public domain.

Printed in the United States of America.

ISBN: 9781545613276

TABLE OF CONTENTS

Introduction..............................ix
Dedication...............................xiii
Acknowledgements........................xv
Preface..................................xvii

1. "Lights Out"........................... 1
2. Facing My Fears, While Hearing Hers..... 17
3. Uncertainty About What She May Say..... 29
4. Am I To Blame? Could This Have Been Prevented?........................... 39
5. When To Listen & When To Talk?........ 51
6. Don't Use It Against Me................ 57
7. Truth Or Just Tried It? Therapy Or Just Her Time?........................... 63

8. So, Did You Tell Your Dad? Or, Should I Tell Him? 77
9. Return Visits to the BLACKROOM ("Marriage Enrichment") 97
10. Life After the BLACKROOM 109

INTRODUCTION

Someone has created a "how to" manual for what seems like everything under the sun; however I have yet to locate the manual specifically for PARENTING. I was sure it would be a subtitle right under the book "101 Things You Should Know Before Marriage". You see, I had a plan. It was not executed perfectly, because it changed often, even still, I had a plan. My plan was to be married, spend a few years building a relationship with my husband, and then become a parent. Be that as it may, I became pregnant on my honeymoon, and building the marital relationship coincided with building a relationship with my first-born child. Additionally, I guess someone should have told me that the relationship building part never ends, but rather, becomes more congested when parenting is attached.

When I married and had my first child it was never my intention to write a book around the discussion of relationships between mothers and daughters. It is funny to me that when you have your first child there's no operation manual that comes along with children, providing instructions on the roles, rules, or expectations that your child will have for you as a parent. Yet, somehow you find it within yourself to "step-up to the plate". You become a person who quickly, and most times naturally, steps-up to represent, guide, counsel, and govern the life of this other individual. It does not matter how you feel about yourself, your abilities, strengths or weakness's; as you must become strategically informed and present. This little person is depending on you for their survival. I had to mentally digest just what my role should be. I became overwhelmed with a barrage of questions. Is this a challenge suited for me… motherhood? What if I am not ready? What if I have made major mistakes in my

INTRODUCTION

life? What if I have been a poor decision maker and lacked the ability to adequately prepare myself over nine months for at least 18 years of responsibility that does not go away?

Well, herein lies the concept of this book. It is our attempt at trying to figure the relationship all out. This book is our attempt at not only getting to know one another, but to use what we find out as tools in building a strong, healthy Mother-Daughter relationship. Like most parents, I wanted things to be better, different and stronger than any relationship I had ever experienced. Whether you have children or not, the fact that we all have had a Mother in our lives, and have experienced relationship building on some level; you will "get it".

I was not looking for perfection, heck-no! This is my child… and needless to say, she by no means came from perfect parents, who had come from a perfect mother and daughter relationship. Yet, that did not stop me from wanting to try to make this my "trophy" relationship. Like really, I had big dreams for this new "doll baby" I was given from God. I think you are feeling where this is going.

Therefore, seamless yet NOT flawless has always been my unspoken desire. To be perfectly honest, my daughter JaLisa (affectionately known as Gigi) is the initiator of those words. I had so many thoughts and ideas, but because it is not exclusively my experience I wanted her input. This book is about our relationship building experiences, so I asked her to give me what she thought would make a good "caption" or summarizing sentence to this book. She immediately replied; "Keys to building an imperfect, yet flawless Mother-daughter Relationship". My reply: Wow!! This "doll baby" is alive and well. She has needs, opinions, and aspirations which she plans to challenge me at assisting her with to the end of time. I am still not sure if I can measure up to her expectations. Fortunately, I have learned that none of these concerns matter anymore. I have to think, act and respond not only for myself, but also for her. Thus begins our journey.

DEDICATION

This book is dedicated to the memory of my Father, Bishop E.M. Thorpe, Sr. Everything I produce is a representation of the amazing love you poured into me. You loaded me daily with "life-words" of how special I was to you. Your life example fossilized my heart to love and serve God until I see you again. I live to love daily because of your love.

ACKNOWLEDGEMENTS

To my Husband, the Father of my two amazing children, without you James W. Vaughn, Jr., none of this would have been possible. You are my love!

To my daughter JaLisa (*"Ja" James and Lisa*) Eugenia-Chaye Vaughn, you are the reason for this writing. Your life will never again be defined by me according to your age, size, failures or successes. You are my one and ONLY Daughter, whom I love, value, and am continually amused by your constant growth.

To my son, Carrington Eugene Vaughn, "The King". You and I did not have "THE BLACKROOM EXPERIENCE". However, nothing will ever replace our kitchen "Stool Talks". You have taught me so much about the process of boy to manhood. "Stool Talk" is the next book in this series of crucial conversations with parents. I love you!

To my mother, Dr. Lola M. Thorpe, the epitome of Motherhood. I thought you had reached the highest elevation possible by simply being my mother, until I became a wife and mother. My children could have never received a greater gift than you as their grandmother. YOU ARE OUR QUEEN!

To my "Writing Coach", Cheryl "Gurly" Edmonds (IGLLYU), there are no words to express my appreciation for how you stood with me, supported, and encouraged me to finally write for myself. Thursdays will never be the same, it is forever a designated "writing day", divinely given from God to us.

PREFACE

Upon completing my Master's degree in English from Carnegie Mellon University in Pittsburgh, Pennsylvania I was told that I had officially become a Rhetorician, someone who should never lose an argument. They taught me how to quickly learn, assess and be prepared for audiences of any age, race, gender and political views. They even taught me how to code someone's words while they were speaking. I mean, I totally believed that I had the upper hand in any conversation. Wrong! They did not tell me how much additional work, strategy and effort would be needed to effectively engage in discourse with someone who had come from me has my traits, may possess my personality and also controls my hearts strings (all of them). Parenting is the exception to all rhetorical rules.

For the past 15 years, I have focused my skills as a Technical Writer on assisting others at gathering, organizing and sharing their thoughts in written documents. Most times this included writings in the form of a training manual, assisting readers at learning a specific concept through its content. Now the time has come to produce for myself. I have worked exceptionally hard to write a book that is not technical, yet provide the reader with specific content that can be used as a tool box-with the type of tools that can be applied repeatedly, ones that keep on producing, in all relationships where one desires to build, with hopes of positive outcomes.

This book is not to be read as a "quick-fix", although woven within it you will find many answers, solutions, ideas, questions, possibilities, practices, and disciplines. It is a handbook on being INTENTIONAL

PREFACE

with what you have been given and whom you have been given. You may grab nuggets, pieces, chunks, or just seeds. Whatever you choose, be sure to use it and begin from where you are with what you have. No, it is not too late. You can begin today; you can begin with this book. Now, **"LIGHTS OUT"**!

CHAPTER 1
"Lights out"

After many years of having plenty of "me time," I found myself losing more and more of that luxury. Redirection of my personal time was mandatory since the birth of my baby girl, JaLisa. No longer was I able to come home, relax (for at least an hour) before cooking dinner for my family or eating what had been prepared. Her birth was the end of my stopping by a few clothing stores after work, for a little "retail therapy". Changing my clothes from business attire into "couch potato" wear was swiftly moved down my after-work to-do list. Instead, I left work focused on how I was going to beat the heavy traffic in order to make it to the daycare prior to its closing. My infant daughter needed my attention and she demanded it in her own little way. Surprisingly, this was a drastic transition for me.

I thought that I would adapt to these transitions during her infancy. The best way I can describe it is by using the metaphor of a theatrical play. Just when I thought I had changed over to act one in my virtual play, "THE PARENT PRACTICES", I was dismayed that it was only the rising of the curtain, not even the prelude to the first act. I unquestionably concluded that my transitions were lagging and required my total focus. Once I refocused, I smoothly stepped out of the door of infancy and into the grand finale of parenting, scene one.

Have you ever felt like someone wanted to tell you something, but they did not know where to start? Well, that is what I was feeling daily. Gi, as I occasionally call her, started out being very, very shy as a young girl. She seemed to be holding on to so much inside. I tried to make conversations with her while instructing, guiding, and maybe some yelling or nagging. Most people would have put all of those words under the umbrella of "parenting," but for me they are slightly different. Webster's dictionary defines parenting as "to be or act as a mother or father to someone" and "the process of taking care of children until they are old enough to take care of themselves…" Neither of these definitions encompass what I felt like my role was to my daughter.

First, I do not *act* like a parent, I *am* a parent. Second, she was between ages 8 to 10 years old, the ages where she could pretty much take care of herself. She was outwardly mature, could cook, clean around the house; she could keep up her personal hygiene, and had a great support system in order to acquire anything materialistic that she needed. Despite all her mature attributes, inside there was a little girl who still had lots of questions, concerns, fears, secrets, and reservations about life.

Knowing this, I began to contemplate how to get inside of this person who had spent 8 long months inside of me (yes, she was premature). I started thinking that maybe I should already know the answers to the ponderings in my mind. My next consideration was that something might be wrong with her. Had my prior life of depression, anxiety, obesity, being an introvert, use of drugs and alcohol have affected her somehow, either physically or emotionally? Maybe someone had done something to her when neither her father nor I was around. I was really, really beginning to trip; I was sending myself into a panic attack of blame, guilt, and shame.

To end this cycle of worrying, I knew it was time to bring in some form of intervention for myself. Who better to start with than her father? Somewhat apprehensive, I swallowed my pride of being the most prepared mother with all the answers. At least, I thought I had all the answers to my own questions. This discussion should be easy. I began with, "Honey (the name I affectionately call my husband Jimmy, when I need his full attention), can I ask you a question; but promise me you will not judge me?" "Why would I judge you?" he replied with a smirk. "Whatever!" I answered sarcastically, then proceeded to tell him all my concerns.

Being that he is her father, and spends as much time with her as I, surely he could assist me. I needed him to calm my fears, and bring a halt to my random, revolving thoughts. He should have known that I was feeling guilty, as if "we" had done something wrong or allowed something wrong to be done to her. Well, that was not quite the case. He simply responded with, "Honey, she is fine. You really should stop tripping." That was not the answer I anticipated, his reply did not comfort me.

The lack of satisfaction with his reply provoked the continuation of my search for how to get my daughter to communicate with me. Next stop was to share with my mother. Surely she had the perfect answer for me.

She had six children, (all with completely different personalities), 18 grandchildren and 5 great grandchildren. My mother and I talked daily; it would be easy to share my concerns one by one with her. In short, one day while we were already talking, I asked my Mother if she thought something was wrong with my relationship with JaLisa? I asked her if she had noticed that JaLisa appeared to be an introvert more when I was around…? Honestly, I did not know how to ask her about the things I was extremely concerned about. Without me asking the right questions, the right way, she listened. You see, to know my mother is to love her, fully accepting that she will always first listen to you, then offer her guidance with one, maybe several stories of what her experiences had been in raising her children. This time, most of the stories she shared with me were about me. By the second story she had shared, it started sounding like I was pretty much the same as JaLisa when it came to communication. I started to think that my situation was not too bad after all. Maybe I should be happy. JaLisa was not half as bad as my mother portrayed me. I am chuckling now because I can visualize this entire conversation. Then, by way of a question, she responds. "What did Jimmy say about your concerns with JaLisa?" and "Did you try to talk to her?" Again, a reply I was not expecting. "Yes, and yes Mom. I have done all of that," I replied. Her conclusion was, she did not feel anything was wrong with JaLisa. As I was about to persist, she interrupts me, saying "Lisa, maybe she is just quiet?" Though her thoughts caused me to pause, that notion still did not sit well with me.

Not long after my discussion with my mother, I walked into my parents home to pick up my children. Sitting at the kitchen table were my Mom, my Dad and JaLisa. All I heard was plenty of conversation and a lot of laughter (which was pretty much the norm with my Dad around). However, JaLisa was fully engaged with the festivities. This was pleasant to see and hear; nonetheless I was feeling a little left out.

Why was I feeling this way? Was it because Jimmy and I were working out of town during the week and both JaLisa and Carrington (my son) had to spend their weekdays with my parents? Of course, we were both so very grateful for their support and assistance. Yet, this did not allow the quality or quantity time I desired to spend building my relationship with my children. What if it was more intricate than anything I could speculate? Maybe I was feeling a void in my life from the past? I began to think about my own personal insufficiencies from the past. For example, as a young girl I often felt "rejected" by others. Back then, my definition of rejection was more like me not fitting into a conversation, not feeling comfortable in a specific group, or even that EVERYONE was talking negatively about me behind my back (shallow thinking). After much maturing my definition of rejection is much closer to Webster's dictionary, although it may still be infiltrated with an enormous amount of emotions. Shazzam! The lights in my head come on. Like a bolt of lightning two realms collide. I think I get it! My void, was mere jealousy. Every time I walked into my parents home and saw JaLisa talking, laughing - joyfully as well as willingly - I felt left out. I was having feelings of rejection. Her happiness was taking me back to a sad place, instead of my being excited that she was not the person that I used to be. Wow! I just grabbed my chest. Still now while writing this book old emotions emerge. I cannot believe I just put those words in black and white! With that said, it is out there, I can exhale and move forward. That was many years of compounded emotions, now released in an abyss, because certainly it does not fit anywhere else.

I am now convinced that it was all in my head and my heart. Every time I came to my parents home to get the kids, JaLisa and my Mother were talking, laughing and enjoying themselves. This is the picture I had conjured up-an abstract portrait stroked with blurred lines of anxiety, distressed and tormented, because of guilty feelings for leaving them while traveling for work. Again, I say, most parents would have been ecstatic to see this, but noooo, not me. Needless to say, I then felt like I had a greater problem; maybe she did not feel comfortable talking to me, maybe I was not an approachable parent, maybe I should quit working and spend more time trying to parent? My mind was spinning.

Finally, I did what I should have done initially and that was ASK GOD about it, pray. I generally rely on my spiritual connection with God. He knows EVERYTHING! He knows me- all my concerns, my fears and my worries, even before I ask. He also knows JaLisa-who she is, who she will become, and how she will be processed to becoming. He knows why He created her and why He made me to be a Mother to her. I am sure you are thinking this is a "no-brainer" Lisa; prayer should have been your first plan of action. I must admit, for some reason, in parenting prayer was not my first action.

"LIGHTS OUT"

This is when I believe my relationship with God became extremely personal. Like never-before I acknowledged that I needed Him. I prayed, praised and worshipped Him more. This was so very important to me; therefore, I knew it was important to Him.

One day it hit me like a ton of bricks! Since I cannot seem to be less emotional, by hiding my facial expressions; maybe if I could shield my physical countenance, my fears, my wanting to be a "perfect parent" (as if one exist), she may feel free to be open as well as honest with me. I was getting distraught, I had to figure out where and how this could take place, hhhmmmm? In my mind, I commenced weighing the pro and cons. My adversities were, I worked out of town, she had school during the day, our weekends were filled with Carrington's sports, Jimmy coming in town and church. Yet, despite these variables, I was feeling quite hopeful. Thank you God, I have figured out "the what" and "the when", I am just missing one piece, "the how"? Two out of three is not bad. "God please lend a hand; I need a little more information with a little more direction to complete the puzzle." This relationship building time is going to require a considerable amount of divine time and strategy, with much INTENTIONALITY.

Intentionality indeed! This was all about building a relationship with my first born, my daughter. I had wanted this experience for years. I read a passage one day written by Mitch Albom that said; *"There is no experience like having children. There is no substitute for it. You cannot do it with a friend. You cannot do it with a lover. If you want the experience of having complete responsibility for another human being, and to learn how to love and bond in the deepest way, then you should have children."* This is the EXPERIENCE I desired.

As time went on I realized that I was being purposeful, but not quite intentional. By that I mean, I had in mind the relational experience I wanted, but I

"LIGHTS OUT"

was missing the preplanned process to reach or acquire what I wanted. I needed a "game plan".

Then, one day while sitting alone with just JaLisa and myself (Jimmy and Carrington were probably at a practice or game), the plan began to emerge. Without thinking about bonding or relationship building, she and I were lying on the bed, all the lights out, watching television. I noticed her talking a little more about the show we were watching. Peculiarly, the conversation seemed to have turned. She started asking me questions. Eventually, the show was off, somehow the television was too. The room was black. Howbeit, the conversation continued. The questions kept rolling, but they began to get deeper, more personal, more like what I had envisioned as a "Mother and Daughter" duo. Suddenly, I became fearful, like OMG! "What if I say the wrong thing?" But no, I had prayed for this Moment and God had answered me. The room was black. Certainly God would not leave me out here like this, with no answer or the wrong answer. I found myself relaxing. My breaths were steady and I was feeling no anxiety. She talked, shared, and ask questions as I laid and listened. I was not searching for words, or answers, I was simply listening.

Amazing to me, what I was learning with the lights out in a totally BLACKROOM was bigger, far beyond my mere intentions. I was learning how to LISTEN, and my daughter was the teacher.

It felt GREAT! I believe I was either learning or perfecting the art and skill of LISTENING. Wow! What a significant stride we had made. Of course, I took it further. I wanted to know more about what made the difference in this day, this time, this setting that caused my daughter to open-up to me. I was diligent and focused in my thinking, I came to a conclusion. I resolved that with the lights out, in this BLACKROOM, my position as "mother" was in some way rendered powerless. It appeared to me that JaLisa felt empowered. It was all her world with my presence being a safety net for her feelings to flow out; spewing all the words she had shelled.

I wanted to spend as much time listening as possible. I know it would probably take me double the time to recall, unpack, deposit and compartmentalize all that she had relinquished. What will happen after this conversation ends? If I were to have a repeat performance, how would I recall the events of this night? How could I yield the same or prayerfully, better results? I was attempting to examine the signs. Was it the show we were watching, the specific room in my house? About to travel down the wrong path again, thinking way too much of the process, I returned to my resolve. Just as God had allowed the perfect situation the first time, He would, when necessary, allow it to happen again. All I needed to think about was how I would avail myself to the needs of my daughter; maybe find the right position to comfortably become a log. Yes, a log; motionless, not thinking ahead, and quiet. Quiet enough to listen and learn.

As parents, we sometimes feel powerless. Nevertheless, this lack of forward movement, seeming like temporary paralysis, should not propel us into a cyclonic state of hopelessness, frustration, misery, or defeat. But rather, lead you to continual relief through your consistent commitment to intentional relationship building versus the dreamy expectation that relationship maturation will simply transpire because you are a parent.

CHAPTER 2

"Facing My Fears, While Hearing Hers"

Yes, I have FEARS! This is not a phrase that most people either young or old would admit. Yet, I will venture to say everyone has some form of fear of something or someone. Although few in number, my fears do occasionally materialize in different situations, but always provoked by something new or an uncertainty. Generally, life uncertainties are the greatest provoker of my fears. Facing situations that I seemingly have absolutely no control over somehow harvests fear in me that alters my ability to function in my God-given purpose. I can only compare it to repeatedly driving a common route to work, every day using the same path. Then, on a random day, an early morning dense fog appears. Confident of my destination, I slowly inch my way down the memorized road, but because I cannot see more than 2 feet beyond the hood of my truck nor approximate the blind spots to the left or right of me, I proceed as a stranger on a journey to a place called "nowhere." It is in the illusion of my fogged uncertainties that I must not allow my fears to emerge where trust is required. Whether past or present, fears of life's uncertainties have to be submitted to what is known. Constantly I must remember to render my fears to the one who is in control of everything, God. However, as a parent I am noticing as my children get older, that I seem to be losing or overcoming many fears only to take on others. Despite the urge to avoid my fears, I am challenged to face them in order to make myself available to hearing, accepting, and assisting my children with theirs. This may sound like an impossibility, but it is a necessity. Yes, just one more additional thing to do in this parenting journey. I was starting to feel like the scripture in the Bible (Galatians 2:20 AMP) which says "I have been crucified with Christ, it is no longer I who lives, but Christ…" This life of mine was quickly becoming not about me. I don't know if I like this. I mean, I am still physically alive. I do exist…

You, too, may want to ask yourself this question, "How do I as parent, mentor, or friend, face my fears while simultaneously hearing the fears of others?" My questions had come to be crystal clear. Questions such as: "How was I going to unselfishly listen to the fears of my daughter, while knowing nestled deep in me remained fears of my own, the bulk of which had much to do with parenting her?" I found myself daily developing more fears concerning her life. I am going to launch out and be brutally honest with you and share some of these fears simply because I am confident that you too may have experienced at least one of these fears while raising a daughter. If not, you can thank me later for the "heads-up".

The list looked something like this: between the ages of 8 years old until today, I have personally struggled with being overweight. When I was in elementary school the kids were so obnoxiously mean, as they tend to be today. MY FEAR: People typically stereotype obese individuals as being lazy, not having a winning personality, and not athletic or active. MY FEAR FOR HER: I was staunch in my resolve that JaLisa was not going to experience this situation, because this is one thing that could be controlled. I worked tenaciously to ensure her relief from the "mean people", fat jokes, and demeaning offenses that I had encountered. I took absolute responsibility for seeing to it that she was physically "common." I made every provision for certainty that she would not be too big, and not too small. However, it seemed I had taken no account of her diminishing self-esteem in the process. Weight was a fixation for me. I became a manic regarding every particle she ingested. Can you imagine how irritating I must have been not only to her, but others as well? Shameful is what I am feeling even now. I took no account for the fact that she was totally oblivious to my reasoning for denying her any random eating pleasures. She could eat no potato chips, and definitely no second plates. What was I thinking? Clearly the only answer is that I was thinking about MY FEARS, while irresponsibly ignoring her feelings? This was wrong on many levels.

JaLisa attended the same school district I attend from second grade through twelfth grade. When I attended, there was little diversity-only about five Black girls in the entire school, and three of them lived in a nearby homeless shelter for youth. Outside of the racial lines of divide, these girls were additionally labeled negatively merely because they did not reside in the community, even worse they were bused from the inner city. You see, to be included in this group, the unspoken was that you and your parents must live on certain streets, look like them and be very involved in ancillary school activities. Sadly to say, from my attendance up until JaLisa's entrance, the diversity had not progressed. No need to say more about that. At this point, it is ok to ask or even wonder why I would place my child in such a perpetuating atmosphere? My response would be that the academic rating of the school district state-wide was excellent. All five of my siblings along with my two nieces have graduated from there. So, despite the lack of diversity, the opportunity to acquire a great education, accompanied with a conducive learning environment, yielded good fruit. Those were enough reasons to undertake the system again. I not only received a good education, but also developed a strong persevering attitude. The value received was worth the price of being daunted. This opposing environment bordering on cynicism, positively provoked my desire to learn, therefore catapulting me into a realm of self-confidence and cultural competency that positioned me for life. Yes, indeed, I wanted this for my children. It was a process that I decided was worth the pain.

A prevalent part of the process involved my feeling excluded and rejected in school. I think I tried to live out their perception of me by becoming a "bully." Why not? I was fat, I was Black, and in that environment, it appeared to be the best recourse. MY FEAR: Even though I survived the stereotyping of others as a young girl, my child may not have the emotional capacity to do the same. Surely I will bequeath no consent to the casting of this esteem-devouring stigma to my daughter. My issues are not permitted to bleed into her life, at school, at home or in any area of her life. Be that as it may, she remained in the district.

I was not only teased in school, but at home amongst my siblings. There was ongoing emotional taunting of my being overweight. As a matter of fact, everywhere I went people seemed to have something negative to say concerning my weight. After so long, I carried a "monkey on my shoulder," presuming people were thinking and speaking negatively about me. Or, more likely that I had created my own mental bleeding, internal spillage from my ears, to my brain, creating the belief that people were even that interested. Consequently, I determined even more that my child's life would not mirror this debilitating humiliation. Appearing successful in that endeavor, (in my mind), what did I do but make the situation worse. To cancel my fear of her being overweight, rejected and excluded I controlled everything-and I do mean EVERYTHING that entered her mouth. Anything I thought that led to my being overweight, was immediately denied her. I will summarize again a few examples: no second plates of anything, no potato chips, no eating and going to bed, no non-activity after school and no "fastfood". Now, do not judge me yet. This was my fear, my concern and my way of eliminating her the pain which I had encountered. When would I realize that being her parent did not permit me to being her God?

This went on for several years, until one night JaLisa and I were riding in the car. We were about two

"FACING MY FEARS, WHILE HEARING HERS"

minutes from home, I can remember the Moment as if it were today. It was a dark night, the car completely black inside, and out of nowhere she said, "Mom, can I ask you a question?" and I replied, "Of course, what's wrong?" She responded with a question that forever changed my fear in this area concerning her and myself. My daughter very cautiously asked, "Mom, if I were fat, would you still love me?" After trying to retrieve my heart which seemed to have flown out of the window into the night air, I gasped for breath. Slowly hitting the breaks of my vehicle, I pulled over. This question demanded as well as deserved her having my full attention. I was very happy that it was dark outside and she could not see the tears flowing down my cheeks, or the shocking personal disappointed expression on my face. I grabbed and hugged her while speaking keenly in her ear, "JaLisa, Mommy will always love you, no matter how you look or what you do." A noiseless sobering Moment for us, no more words to be spoken. We remained there embraced for a while. We were both shedding tears at that point. I just kept holding her. I wanted to hold her forever, because I felt as if I had failed her for life. My intentions were on the right street, but not the right house. All I was trying to be was a parent, her Mother; one who loved, protected, developed, encouraged and availed myself to her. I had "epically" failed.

From that day until now I do not speak negatively about her height, weight, body shape or size. I work very intentionally at not even speaking negatively to her concerning my weight. This particular event is when I would say was the beginning of me facing my fears, while hearing hers. What a huge lesson I had learned.

So, I ask again, how do you as a parent simultaneously face your fears, while hearing the fears of your child or any other person? My suggestion: first thing to do is identify your past, maybe even present fears? Then identify your fears as a parent? This question can be asked relating to all relationships of relevance to you. I can only state my fears, this being just one of them. Please note, neither you nor I can possess the power to conquer our fears without confessing them. This warrants concise acknowledgement that the fears are present. THE POWER FOR CHANGE IS IN CONFESSION.

My greatest fear should have begun with these questions, "Am I able to provide her unconditional love? Can I continuously be present in her life active or silent, whether I am requested or not? Will I unselfishly not place my personal past, my fears on her?"

Being overweight was just one fear, but as the years went by many other, now embarrassing, fears emerged. Moving forward, promise me that you will not judge me, and I promise you I am better today.

My quest for unknown fears sounds somewhat like the following: Would my daughter be pregnant as a teenager, ending up with a baby out of wedlock? If that were to happen, how would I be viewed as a Mother? How would I handle her; would I put her out of the house for fear of added financial obligation? What if she were a loose girl, sexually promiscuous, a "whore?" I am dropping my head even while typing these words. I am ashamed at my past thinking. But, you need to know, because some of you have felt the same. Anyhow! What if she became a lesbian (or as my Dad called it, a "bull-dagger")? What if she chose Atheism or a male friend that hated God and His people? I must be honest in this book or I cannot expect for you, JaLisa or anyone else to be honest with yourselves about where you are in your relationships. Honesty is mandatory for THE BLACKROOM EXPERIENCE.

CHAPTER 3

"Uncertainty About What She Might Say?"

Have you ever heard of the television show called "Kids Say the Darnedest Things"? The gist of the show was an adult host would ask kids between the ages of 5-8 years old a series of questions and they would tend to respond in a winsome and funny way. They were not prompted to answer according to what any adult would expect them to say. I thought the show was darling with its innocent questions. Most did not have much to do with "real life" issues, or personal adult problems outside of the kids' understanding. I share this because I would have only hoped for a similar situation when communicating with JaLisa. Yet, I could by no means conjure-up a sandwich size bag of "certainty." There was no way to anticipate what would be said from one **BLACKROOM EXPERIENCE** to another.

As JaLisa was growing older, meeting new people, learning new things and gaining her own personality, the uncertainty about what she may say was also growing. In the beginning of our "Room Rap," which I may hereafter refer to as R&R time, she was between the ages of 6 to 10 years old. She was attending her third elementary school, learning to share, speak for, and defend herself. The multiple schools had much to do with her acquiring an adaptable outlook on people from diverse backgrounds. She did not seem to be negatively affected by the change or transitions, but I knew by watching and listening to her daily that she was bottling up a long list of questions, only to be asked at the most unpredictable as well as inconvenient time. Therefore, I needed to prepare myself. I

"UNCERTAINTY ABOUT WHAT SHE MIGHT SAY?"

thought it might be to my advantage to begin asking her questions, while she was still pondering about how and when. Surely with her growing older, all while adapting to transition after transition of mine, she would question me with some "biggies," once she found the right time.

One of the areas of concern I felt she might have questioned would be, "Why have we been moving around so much, from state to state and house to house?" Now really, as a "wannabe good parent" that question would have never been answered with the real truth. I would not have lied but rather answered around the question. I was taught that some things simply were not necessary to tell your children. Therefore, my behavior in parenting was somewhat synonymous to what I would like to call an "unspoken code of parenting". Remember no instructions or manual came along with the onset of parenting. In my meager attempts for "how to?" I adopted the phrase, "We do what we have to do to make it work." This included a smorgasbord of extreme behaviors and phrases; from "robbing Peter to pay Paul," to arguing quietly with my husband in our bedroom about a parenting decision he made with which I disagreed, then walking out of the bedroom expressionless as if an intense argument had not just occurred or been heard by my children. I did the marital "quiet-fight" in the bedroom as not to cause my children to worry about whatever was worrying us. That said, my adopted phrase, "We do what we have to do to make it work," worked for me. Furthermore, as for me and our house, we did NOT permit children to ask certain questions-especially questions which we as parents were uncertain of, nor did we include them in any part of the household decision-making equation. If you are being provided the necessities of life (love, food, clothing, shelter, more love…) no need for answers to the "how?" Of course, these were all early on personal parental perspectives, not planning ahead for a BLACKROOM EXPERIENCE.

"UNCERTAINTY ABOUT WHAT SHE MIGHT SAY?"

During those early years of my marriage, my husband and I were still trying to figure out our lives. Ok, yes that was fairly after the fact. But, we still had many of our own things we desired to do and be that had not yet occurred. One of those things was deciding in which state we would live. When JaLisa was four years old her father made the decision that we would move to Sacramento, California. JaLisa was about to go to Kindergarten. This relocation would mean she would be leaving the group of people that she was most familiar with since birth; our family, who were great supporters of ours, along with the staff at the daycare located in our church. She spent both weekends and weekdays with these individuals. In an attempt to make a comfortable life for our family, I cannot say that we took much consideration in how this decision would affect JaLisa then or later. I knew I would be working in the field of daycare, therefore I rested assured that she would still be with me every day-all day.

THE BLACKROOM EXPERIENCE

    What I was not confident in was how any of our moves, to hopefully building a better life, would fare with her. I began to have uncertainties that maybe we were being bad examples of stability. Then several years later, while in our R&R time I realized that this is a child who understands beyond her years. I can recall while living in California, I had no one to talk to, but JaLisa. Carrington was only about 3 months old and Jimmy was commuting, still working in Pittsburgh. He was there with the rest of my entire support system. Many days I could not sleep. I would even go as long as a week without three consistent hours of sleep. I was jittery, full of anxiety and non-responsive to my parental responsibilities. I found myself talking to and depending on JaLisa more and more. I was giving her additional responsibility for Carrington along with herself. She was just five years old, but I was teaching her how to cook, clean, load the dishwasher, change Carrington's Pampers and dress him. Inquisitively, one day she asked me, "Mom, where is Dad?" I replied, "He's at grandma's house in Pittsburgh." She

"UNCERTAINTY ABOUT WHAT SHE MIGHT SAY?"

responded, "Oh, well why can't we go there so you don't have to do all of this work?" I paused, trying to muster up an answer; one fitting for a five-year old. Then, I said, "Your Dad has to be there so he can go to work, then he comes here with us on the weekends (not my best answer). Why are you asking me all of these questions?" Yes, I was getting agitated. I do not know if my agitation was with JaLisa's questions or with Jimmy for not being present. She continued the conversation with this adult like conclusion, "Well maybe if we were all together, neither of you would have to work so hard. Because, you keep saying you are tired." This inquiring episode was one of many. My first thought was to just tell her, "You are making a lot of sense little girl. I am tired and have no one else to talk to or share the load with, therefore I am loading you with responsibilities that your Dad would perform, if he were here." Nonetheless, that would have been an excessive response to a child. She was making good sense, asking good question. She deserved an appropriate answer. Turning away from her, acting as if something more urgent requested my attention, I replied in haste; "That's a good question. Call your Dad and ask him."

Another incident comes to mind while sharing this. I spoke earlier of how much responsibility I placed on JaLisa while very young. This parental act was not all bad. She turned out to be extremely dexterous in cooking, very domesticated, and dependable while young. Eventually, we did relocate back to Pittsburgh (as she had so respectfully hinted towards). Finally, we were all under one roof. Life was normalizing itself. JaLisa was getting older, more inquisitive, less burdened by the responsibilities of her mother. Yet, we were unceasing at the maintenance of our seamless random conversations.

One day, after a long, laborious ride home from work in extreme traffic, she began her queries. Query number one: "Mom, when we were in California and Dad was in Pittsburgh, you were always tired. Now we are back with Dad and you are still tired, are you sick?" How was I to answer this seeming cross-examination

"UNCERTAINTY ABOUT WHAT SHE MIGHT SAY?"

from my child? I do not remember my exact reply, but I presume it went something like this, "JaLisa when I say I am tired, it does not really mean tired, like sleepy or sick. Maybe I say that too much. I'm going to watch my words from now on. And, no I am not sick" (again, looking away so as not to make her feel I had brushed her off).

There is nothing worse than the sensation of disappointing your child's expectations of you. Even in the uncertainties, they expect you to minimally act like an adult. I do not know if you do personal evaluations. I did not prior to parenting. Today I am exceptionally acquainted with evaluating all aspects of my persona. From my occasional whining to my daily road rage, from my facial expression in church to my brassy marital disagreements. Why? Because you never know to what or when children are paying attention. So, parent beware!

CHAPTER 4

"Am I To Blame? Could This Have Been Prevented?"

Allow me to walk you through this journey. This journey is all about confronting and dealing with the fear of the unknown, or better yet, the "fear of the fear". Maybe I should begin this chapter preparing you for the "what ifs?" in life, which most often end up with people playing the "blame game" either on each other or solely with themselves.

I think I will just jump in at the end of an R&R. This was the process: we would leave THE BLACKROOM after having our R&R. JaLisa would appear to be happy and satisfied with me as her parent, and even herself for having dumped things she had been holding on to since our last visit. She looked to be free to embrace life more empowered, with confidence that many of her life questions had been answered. On the other hand, I had to continue to be a loving parent and find somewhere to place all the weight she had just shed. I definitely could not hold on to her words, questions or concerns. That would have been way too toxic to handle without me blaming her, myself, Jimmy or God for any of the not-so-positive information she shared. This is where I was prone to cast fault on myself. If I possibly could have answered her questions through my example or through lessons I taught her, much of this could have been prevented. Yet, at that time without a parenting manual, I could only give what I thought best. It was not that the things she questioned were always bad, rather it was my challenge to merely remain focused on not blaming anyone for her questions or concerns. All of this took time; time to hear it, time to place it, and time to heal it. It was necessary that these conversations be in a safe place, never to be brought up again (unless she did the recalling). Along with that, I did not have the capacity to retain it all. Nonetheless, I too was growing.

One BLACKROOM conversation that has continued was my fear of older men being attracted to JaLisa an issue I had as a young girl. The history of this began with me having "grown up in the church". Our church was led by my father who was the Pastor, and my mother who co-pastored alongside him. Our church was known for having what we call Revivals. Back then they would continue anywhere from one week long to sometimes as long as months. My father would invite speakers from far and near, known and unknown, the "real deal" and some "pseudo-preachers". The entire city of "church-goers" would attend in support of each and every event. The services were always vibrant and celebratory. As a child, I enjoyed these experiences. Very few guests were monotonous or humdrum. Most were extremely charismatic, leaving their listeners desiring more. This was the reason why many of the services were extended.

It may be surprising that as a child I enjoyed this, but at the time my parents were like "Church-Celebrities." They both were very hospitable, outgoing, and totally engaged in their faith. Both were charismatic in demeanor, while attracting a diverse group to themselves individually.

My Mother has always lived a principle-based life, never toeing-the-line of reproach. She has consistently "preached" the necessity of living a balanced life. Too much of anything was too much in her eyes. Folly and fun have never been prevalent in her character. Her temperament is to share her convictions through her strong stance, while extending a hand of correction in love. My Father was totally opposite, which is probably why their bond lasted so long. I would say he lived somewhat under a more gracious base. Often full of folly, fun and fashionable, he was the "Hollywood

Bishop." He loved God, people, church, church and, oh yes, did I say Church? Life was church and church was his life-good ole-fashion church. He brought energy, excitement and spontaneity to every service. All of this because you never could guesstimate what would come out of his mouth. He loved all, liked many and tolerated few. A mixture of people were drawn to him as well as he to them. Making friends everywhere he went, of all denominations, he was determined to bring them back to his local church to share with his congregants. This is where the conflict would take place. Put simply, not all who he invited were the best fit or had the best intentions. Some came focused on the assignment of sharing the Gospel of Jesus Christ. Others came for the "fishes and loaves." Then there were a few who came for the "pickings" just to prey on the innocent. Warning JaLisa of these wolves in sheep's clothing was my primary objective.

I did not mean to frighten her of all men of the cloth, knowing not all of them were imitators of the faith. When I say imitators of the faith these men abused their spiritual authority as well as their power to seduce young girls, even boys in the church. It was and is diabolical manipulation, leaving their prey lost in daze of questions as to why this happened to them. I simply wanted to raise precautionary flags, hoping to prevent a repeat of my worst experiences. I wanted to ensure that if any of them attempted to seduce her, she would tell me all, confident that she would be heard, believed and supported. Once these imitators think you will not tell anyone of their offense, they have you "GAME OVER," they win. Looking in retrospect today, I would say my efforts to protect went quite a bit further than intended. Back peddling is no longer an option when some damage is done.

As happy as I was to be spending quality amounts of time with my daughter, each BLACKROOM Experience presented me with its own level of anxiety. Each visit created an overwhelming amount of stress for me. This stress precipitated recalling of the words

"AM I TO BLAME? COULD THIS HAVE BEEN PREVENTED?"

in the song recorded by the singing group Temptations, "It was just my imagination, running away with me…" I am sure these emotions could have been contained. However, never having a clue of what JaLisa would say caused my brain cells to shoot out sparks in my head similar to the 4th of July. This occurred especially when things in her life or in our family would not be going so well. My best description is most like watching fireworks, never knowing if they were going to come out big and beautiful across the sky or just a boom with no spark of color or thrill.

I wanted to believe that at the end of each visit, we had conquered all the cares of life. When we turned on the lights ending a BLACKROOM EXPERIENCE, I felt like the "Mother of the year". Surely no one else was getting the results that I was with their daughter. Just the opposite was true. I was more like "Mother of the Moment." Then, every following BLACKROOM request was another parent panic incident for me. Our experience would begin like this, JaLisa would say,

"Mom can we talk, in the dark?" My heart seemed to drop to the floor. I tried to not show it in front of her, but oooooohhh the fear and agony those words brought me. Then, between the time she asked to talk and our actual visit, was the time I spent creating the mental 4th of July, fireworks ablaze. I tried to guess at what the problem could be this time. I did not give space to the fact that she was growing, maturing, experiencing life and with each of those levels came new unexpected, often puzzling concerns, not necessarily problematic.

I can be quite dramatic when it comes to the reluctances in my life. So, at this juncture I am curious. How do you react during your "in-between-time" as it relates to unknown relationship talks? Are you immediately excited for the opportunity to hear, positioned in a positive posture, confident that all is well? Or, would you say you were more like me? Awaiting this time as one peering into the cloudy sky expecting the cloud of blame to hover over you; exploding tiny pieces of your parental mistakes all around, creating a great mess to be cleaned up only by the "want-to-be perfect" mother/friend/etc.? You do not have to answer, but if not, you pretty much have your answer. UNCERTAIN, yes like me. Sometimes I felt that at any given Moment these pieces of the exploded cloud would cover even smother me. Maybe that is what I wanted to happen instead of hearing what she would say next. You may now be asking yourself, "I thought this is what she wanted." That would be the correct question to ask. I was asking the very same question about myself, to myself. "I thought this is what you wanted Lisa, right?"

The reality is that once I entered the room whatever happened was going to happen. I was wasting precious time haggling over the "what ifs". I had to constantly remind myself that this is what I wanted, desired and asked God to cause to happen. There was no blaming happening as I anticipated, only the mental game that I continued to play on myself. However,

I did learn much in this process, which lessened my stress as I continued returns to the BLACKROOM. The first thing was, do NOT anticipate the worst. I realized and so must you, that before we were a parent/mentor/caregiver/etc., we are human. We had questions, concerns, maybe even worries that we wished to share with someone. This someone would probably be a person who did not have preconceived thoughts of who we were, what we were going to share or even how they were going to respond. This person would be a good listener, non-judgmental, did not hold grudges and was not a "know-it-all".

I learned that my ability to have the "right" answer did not matter. There was no one at fault. If there was a problem I had to know without a doubt that it was a part of our process. Because it was a part of our life process it had to happen. We had to go through it and nothing or no one could have prevented us from the experience.

"AM I TO BLAME? COULD THIS HAVE BEEN PREVENTED?"

What happens in us when we anticipate the worst? We create what I call "fearing the fear," and this is absolutely not emotionally healthy. What happens to dreams or even nightmares that are deferred? Maybe it was never real, therefore will never happen. Is it ok to leave questions unanswered? Of course, it is ok not to have the answers all the time. Even so, never ever allow that to stop you from listening or being present in a life that depends on you. Yes, questions, questions, questions. But keep reading, I promise you that either your answers are forthcoming or the peace of not knowing will be released in you, allowing you to rest in that resolve.

HARLEM

By LANGSTON HUGHES

What happens to a dream deferred?
Does it dry up
like a raisin in the sun?

THE BLACKROOM EXPERIENCE

Or fester like a sore—
And then run?
Does it stink like rotten meat?
Or crust and sugar over—
like a syrupy sweet?
Maybe it just sags
like a heavy load.
Or does it explode?

CHAPTER 5
"When To Talk And When To Listen?"

All my life I would have considered myself a good listener. Well that was until I had my daughter. It is so funny to me how much I have learned from a child. While in college I minored in Communications. One of the key lessons that I will never forget was nonverbal communication. Nonverbal communication is defined as communication without the use of spoken language. Nonverbal communication includes gestures, facial expressions, and body positions (known collectively as "body language"), as well as unspoken understandings and presuppositions, and cultural and environmental conditions that may affect any encounter between people. Recently, because of my desire to communicate more effectively with JaLisa as well as others, I have been practicing better listening skills. Research suggests that only 5 percent effect is produced by the spoken word, opposed to 45 percent by the tone, inflection, and other elements of voice. The same research shows that 50 percent of effect is produced by body language, movements, eye contact, etc. You may wonder if this information is correct, why was I practicing better listening skills? I was wondering the same until I came to realize that listening has as much to do with my heart as it does with my ears. The research I found redirected my listening skills. As a parent, I determined that I needed to hear as much of what my child was not saying, as well as every word that she spoke. Her shy, reserved behavioral language from her heart should have been ear-piercingly blatant to mine. I learned that her intermittent verbal transmissions were nothing in comparison to the amplified unspoken. This knowledge I placed in my depository

"WHEN TO TALK AND WHEN TO LISTEN?"

of skills, never to be consigned to oblivion. Persuaded that there was more to this listening skill than words and discourse, I continued my quest, confident that I was "barking up the *right* tree."

To me listening is an art and a skill that totally involves nonverbal communication. You can be present, face-to-face with someone and not be listening to a word they are saying. One of my favorite definitions for listening is to be alert, ready to hear. I have concluded through the process of parenting that the many years I prided myself on listening to people, I was simply present while they were talking. My daughter JaLisa, through my BLACKROOM EXPERIENCES, has taught me how to effectively listen. Our experiences have taught me how to be "all in" when communicating. I now find myself handling all my relationships this way. We are either going to be "all in" when communicating-or not at all. I no longer listen while watching television, texting on the phone or gazing on my computer. No space to multi-task when I am supposed to be listening to someone; therefore, I am now expecting the same.

Following the first few visits to THE BLACKROOM I must admit two things. Number one: I spent more time hearing and listening than providing parental guidance, instructions or any information. Number two: if I remember correctly, I cried every time. Ok, once again please no judgement of me or expecting me to know why? That would require me to be stretched prostrate on the couch of a certified therapist to be figure out. Have you ever gone through an uncertainty that each time you even thought about it you began to well up with strong emotions, teetering on the verge of tears? How about experiencing this emotion and you had no thoughts that provoked it? I'm guessing it was more like that for me. However, I did get better, stronger and more resilient with each visit. Eventually I learned to listen, navigating my emotions kind of like a skilled experienced captain of my own cruise ship.

"WHEN TO TALK AND WHEN TO LISTEN?"

Once I felt this skill had developed sufficiently the next task was to graduate with honors to a more advances course in listening to what I felt, sensed or presumed as the real concern behind the critical conversation. Can I hear what she is not saying, can I feel what she wants to say, and can I sense the delicate emotions amplified by her silence? That is Listening! My assignment will not cease as long as she lives. As it relates to listening I will always seek to perfect my how to and what to? Most importantly, through the light of listening, I have learned the "when to".

CHAPTER 6
"Don't Use It Against Me"

As an adult I have had a few friendships where I became vulncrable beyond measure. Maybe I was emotionally weak at that time or simply trying out my "trust factor" on others. Whichever it may have been, there were times when I have disclosed EXTREMELY personal things within relationships to people who should not have had that level of access. Some of the Moments I wish had never happened or that at the beginning of the conversation I had an imaginary electronic muzzle that knew to activate when I was just about to get comfortable and spew out information I would later regret. Unlike my past relationships, I now had to use my "trust factor" tactics in a more constructive way. My new task was to ensure that while in the BLACKROOM JaLisa felt safe to spew out whatever she desired (of course in a respectful manner) with "no worries" or regret.

She may differ, but I feel that one of the key benefits we experienced in the BLACKROOM is that I was not permitted to bring the discussed conversation up later. Whatever we had discussed was just that, discussed. She shared and I responded (when necessary). Anything that I did not say at that time could NOT be spoken of in the light-unless she brought it up. Really? Now how hard do you think that was for me as a parent? First of all, I did not fully process the conversation until after the lights were on. For example, one visit to THE BLACKROOM (*and I am permitted to share in this setting*) she shared with me about a time when she was in school and another student (whom she considered a friend) asked for her answers to a test. JaLisa had her cell phone (which was not permitted

"DON'T USE IT AGAINST ME"

by the school) and during the class and/or the test, she texted the answers to this girl. The result- she was caught by her teacher! Oh, and by the way, did I mention that she has always been a horrible "sneak". The background is, JaLisa was just entering high school, spreading her "friendship" wings, meaning she was trying to find "her group" or where she fit in and with whom. Needless to say, her initial choice was not such a good decision. She would have done better to have "clipped her wings off", than to have connected to this person. Either way she was not going very far making those reckless choices. Not comfortable with the school's no cell phone policy, I had allowed her to take her cell phone to school. I believed her when she said, "Mom, we cannot even get a phone signal in the school unless we are outside of the building." That was enough for me, therefore allowing her to break the school rules. My logic behind that decision was based on the fact that she had limited access (so she said…), the many bad things happening in schools all over the country, and our experience during the terrorist attack of September 11, 2001. A time when I could not reach her through the school and was left to worry frantically. That was a very frightening feeling, and I committed to never let that happen again. However, my allowing her to take the phone to school (break the rules) and JaLisa's motives for wanting the phone during the day were totally opposite. Yet, because I had made a bad decision of supporting her in breaking the rules, I held a bit of guilt in this fiasco.

So, when in the BLACKROOM she began to talk about that incident. She told me the *whooooole* story, or should I say the "true story". She first talked about the cell phone signal. Thinking back, I cannot believe I fell for that... (chuckling) Eventually she said "Mom, I did not tell you the truth about the cell phone signal in the school". I responded asking her why the lie and what was the truth? She responded by explaining that the kids at school had a way of doing something to the cell phone that would cause a break in the school's system, unblocking the blocked signal. I am now shaking my head, because that sounds like more "crap talk" that I fell for. She went on to ask me, "Mom, didn't you notice that when I needed something I would call you from my cell phone during the school day and I was not calling from the nurse's office or the principal's office?" I hesitated in response, I was starting to get angry. The darkness was definitely of benefit to both of us at that Moment. The Mom in me was kicking in and I was about to light into her. I think she may have felt some thumps in the mattress of the bed. It was either my heart beating rapidly or she heard my breaths getting deep, louder, more bull like. Quickly she blurted out, "Mom, you said I can tell you ANYTHING in the BLACKROOM and I won't get in trouble." Whew, she was swiftly saved by her "blurt" of reminder. Even in the darkness, she was developing female intuition skills that may have saved her life and our Moment. If she was an adult she could have used the phrase, "What happens in Vegas, stays in Vegas."

What good is it to spend so much quality time working on a relationship listening, growing and learning if when finished, you later bring up all the conversation that you did not approve of, against the person? Imagine that, or even how much worse this would have been especially if you are a parent whose child trusts in your commitment to them simply because it is your word.

CHAPTER 7

"Truth Or Tried It? Therapy Or Just Her Time?"

When I was growing up I recall my mother working judiciously with all six of her children. We were each very different emotionally. Yet my mother had a way of figuring us out individually, compartmentalizing our issues. Then she decided how to handle us separately. I only have two children, one daughter and one son. I cannot fathom going through that process six times, repeatedly following calculated steps with hopes of reaching specific goals for each child.

That strategy seemed to have worked well for my mother. However, for me, her process could not be mimicked. My version was a bit more dramatic. I would think of the worst possible life scenario. Then, I would work backwards from there. I remember when JaLisa was entering her late teens, I would never allow her to hang around girls her age who were unwed mothers. I am not quite sure what my logic was at that time or what I could have possibly been thinking. I was aware that once a girl had begun her menstruation she was able to be impregnated. JaLisa had reached that place. What if her friends who were sexually active expressed their pleasure in having sex, peeking JaLisa's interest to engage? My teenage friends were sexually active and always shared with me in an exciting way the gratification they felt while sexually involved. They sounded mature, like adults; and I did not mind being perceived as adult-like. Maybe my unconscious mind triggered something I had heard as a child; perhaps it was affecting my parenting principles. When I was a teenager I can recall hearing, older people state this myth, "If you touch a woman who was pregnant, you would be pregnant soon after." Therefore, whenever a newly married couple desiring a child would come into the presence of an expecting mother, the older married couples would tell her, "Just rub her belly, and soon you will become pregnant as well." Have you ever heard of such nonsense? Likewise, some would say, "Birds of a feather, flock together." I am sure you have heard that one. My interpretation now being passed onto my daughter, is that if someone were to hang-out around people who were sexually promiscuous, using illegal drugs or not achieving in school, the person who has not engaged in those behaviors would suddenly begin like behaviors. The latter may be easier to perceive as a truth versus the first "myth". All of these superstitious are now ignorant thoughts to me, containing no more truth than the Mother Goose rhyme "The cow jumped over the moon." All of this now considered as humorous nonsense. JaLisa could not get pregnant by befriending or hanging out with a pregnant person. Nor would she abruptly become pregnant by simply holding the baby of someone else. Adopting these erroneous myths as truth was as bad as thinking if a woman ate watermelon with its seeds, she would shockingly come to be an expectant mother not long after. As if insinuating a seed would grow on the inside. At any rate, what was their point? Shaking my head, people have said some crazy things! I am sure you can agree that you have heard at least one of these ridiculous warnings? If not, I am either indirectly telling my age or unintentionally outing the intelligence of the older adults I came into contact with as a youth. Possibly I simply should not have been eavesdropping on the conversation of those adults.

I am extremely delighted that I now know the truth. The "truth" is my daughter and no other female could become pregnant by befriending a pregnant person. The truth is, even if she was having pre-marital sex as a teenager it does not necessarily mean she would eventually become with child. The truth is, fear of my daughter becoming a teenage mother was just a fear, not necessary my ghastliest reality.

Why am I admitting to the lunacy of my fears? It is because I know I am not alone in my occasional absurd thinking, or am I?

I am sharing this because, yes, there were many times that JaLisa portrayed behavior that was considerably circumspect. She was a young girl maturing into the wonderful young lady she is today. The bumps in the road we had to endure on our journey could have altered the relationship we have and the person she has become today.

I often think about an incident we had after people had convinced JaLisa that her physical shape was more appealing than she imagined. JaLisa was in the ninth or tenth grade and was preparing her attire for a school dance. Typically, she would ask my opinion about what to wear, how she looked in certain styles, and the like. For some reason, this time was different.

JaLisa was beginning to no longer be interested in what I thought of how she looked. I believe it was mainly because others were telling her as well as myself, what a great body she had. She said to me, "Mom, can you please call my Godmother and ask her if she would pick out my outfit for the dance?" This took me back for second, and then I replied, "Sure." In the back of my mind I was very clear on what this meant. From my perspective, she did not care about how I would feel as her mother with her change of desire. This may seem frivolous to some, but let me explain how I translated this one request for her Godmother to assist her in her first high school dance outfit. I heard, "Mom, I am getting older and no longer want to dress in clothes that are three sizes too big, simply because you do not want boys or men looking at my body." I heard, "Mom, you have always said that I am shaped just like my Godmother, (which is a compliment) and that you like the things she wears, therefore, it would only make sense if you just have her help you in dressing

"TRUTH OR TRIED IT? THERAPY OR JUST HER TIME?"

me from here on." JaLisa's Godmother was always very present in her life. She saw to it that JaLisa had the newest, most stylish and the "coolest" clothes a young girl could desire. However, she and I frequently disagreed on the correct size as well as the appropriateness of the clothing she provided. Oh my goodness, there was always more than enough, bags and bags of clothes, shoes, coats, and accessories. I would say to her "Kim, JaLisa does not need all of this stuff, please do not buy her anything else." My words did not deter her at all; they may have even incited her. Kim had two daughters who were older than JaLisa, who JaLisa thought highly of. It seemed like she had been studying how Kim had prepared their outfits for their high school events. I did not know at the time that she even paid attention to style at the level of her Godmother and her daughters. It appeared that JaLisa had been waiting for her time. And, I am sure I heard, in that one simple request, "Mom, she also dresses sexier than you, which means I have a much better chance of looking sexier if she is involved." Ok, ok I will stop right there, enough of my insecure, unstable mind "Mom Moments".

Back to my point. There were times when I would take simple situations as I have mentioned and turn them into illusions of my fears. I had a way at twisting a naive request from my daughter into a complex mental fantasy. The truth was not that JaLisa wanted to dress sexy so that boys or men would look at her. Rather, she was growing, trying to find her style, wanting to realize the look that would suit her amongst new peers. If she wore a fitted dress, hitting slightly above the knee, it was not a sign that she was a "fresh" little girl attempting to look like a grown sexy lady. This was not a "red alert" that she was on a path to becoming a strung-out prostitute, walking the streets at night. I am purposefully exaggerating this shallow incident. However, what if I had projected my ill thinking or past personal accusations on my daughter? What if any of us defined our children or any others by the things they have tried, or merely sought to experience? Growth is radical; it is not always a beautiful sight. Transformation can seem tragic, but is not a time to define. The truth is JaLisa "tried it" with me, it was commonly her time. She did not need therapy for her natural maturation into becoming herself. These were some of the things I learned by allowing us to have THE BLACKROOM EXPERIENCE. I came out of the room each time more understanding of the necessity for my personal healing in order that we both could continue to grow. I learned that as important as it is to know the truth and speak truth, the greater challenge comes in what we do with that truth.

The most important question for me continues to be, "What will be done with the truth discovered?" I chose to add this to my tool-kit of parenting skills. The truth is I tried to be the perfect parent, an informed and equipped parent. It is the truth that I will never have all the answers. It is as well the truth that I needed a tool-kit full of resources which I could utilize properly at any given Moment. The tool that was never made available to me could have assisted me in parenting my daughter. Prayerfully, this book will provide the assistance necessary.

Late in my career, I worked for an agency that required all their staff to take a Temperament Analysis. The purpose of the test was that through it we would better learn how to effectively as well as intentionally work with each other, being sensitive to one another's multiplicity of needs. The therapist shared the purpose in giving this particular analysis. The end results would ultimately be awareness of how God sees us from birth to death. Knowing the primary purpose was that we all would grow through this knowledge despite what we think we know individually to be the truth about ourselves. God graces us every day towards who and what He created us to be.

After taking the analysis I was astonished-initially even frightened-by my results. The entire staff met in the conference around the table. The therapist who had administered the test distributed each person their individual results. Walking and talking, he explained to us all that we may not like or agree with our results. He stated that if we had questions concerning our test results, he would be more than willing to meet with us individually. I sat patiently quiet. I began reading my results as soon as his hand was extended in my direction. Before he had an opportunity to put it in my hand I snatched it out of his. I did not mean to be rude, yet I did not want anyone else to get a glimpse. It was almost the behavior one might display in school when the teacher was returning an exam that you are quite sure you had not passed.

As I was reading, I began to well up on the inside with uncontrollable emotion. I am not one to denounce my personal truths, but what I was reading about myself were truths that I had buried deep within the dungeons of my soul. These were truths that only God knew about me. Who unlocked these doors in which there were no keys? How did the basic questions I answered on a couple pieces of paper release such secret files of my life? I could not contain myself another second. Suddenly, I burst into tears, I had only made it to the sixth of thirteen pages. I lost all awareness as to where I was, who was at the table or how to gather myself. There were so many personal truths exposed through that test. I often refer back to it in Moments of vacillation of who God designed me to be. A few Moments after the emotional volcano I had experienced, I felt a freedom and peace come over me like never before. It was out. I had faced, embraced and came to the realization that the truth does make us free indeed. I was free! No more dungeons, dark places or denial. That day changed my life and it changed how I parented. It changed my old thoughts of insufficiency as a parent. I accelerated straight to "Super-Mom." God had cleaned the slate eliminating the desire to bleed my past truths into the life of my daughter. My BLACKROOM EXPERIENCES would soon change. Illumination was coming.

"TRUTH OR TRIED IT? THERAPY OR JUST HER TIME?"

In closing this chapter, I must share with you that once my life emerged out of darkness, I needed security in knowing that my prior parenting skills had not caused irreversible damage to my daughter. I wanted her to know the difference between her truth and her "tried it." I wanted her BLACKROOM EXPERIENCES to shed light to her life.

The truth is I had her take the Temperament analysis at 13 years old, but did not allow her to read it until she was 17 years old-an age where I felt she could understand the test and better understand herself. My initial reason for having her take the test was to provide a tool for me, aiding me in knowing the person I was parenting. I needed to know what God had designed as well as graced my daughter to be so that I would not interrupt His process. Contrary to what I thought JaLisa needed earlier, the truth is we both needed and did receive therapy. Today, we are both better for it.

CHAPTER 8

"Did You Tell Your Dad?" "Or Should I Tell Him?"

It was a Wednesday evening; we had eaten dinner and were winding our day down. As I was moving around in the kitchen, trying to clean up after having a scrumptious dinner with both of my children and my husband (it was a treat to have us all together), I saw out of my peripheral view JaLisa moseying around. She was not focused on anything specific. She was "being" around. When finally, I asked her, "Gi, do you have homework tonight?" She simply replied, "No Ma'am". She continued meandering from one room to another, from the couch to the chair to the kitchen stool, while I was working. Eventually, I said, "Well then, since you seem to have so much time on your hands, come help me with this kitchen…!" Of course, she did not receive that task with joy-in all probability, wishing she had stayed out of my view. She listlessly dragged herself back into the kitchen and started loading the dishwasher. Yes, you are correct if you are thinking she should have asked me, "What would you like me to do, Mom? or "How can I help?" Instead, since she had been paying much attention to my busyness, she knew what she needed to do. We continued in the kitchen for about another 15 minutes, her not saying a word, me trying to figure out why all the lingering this evening.

Dishes were in the dishwasher, pots and pans scrubbed, floor swept, table wiped, but still no words exchanged. Finally, Jimmy and Carrington said goodnight and headed upstairs, leaving JaLisa and me alone. At this juncture, I started to think this was going to be

"DID YOU TELL YOUR DAD?" "OR SHOULD I TELL HIM?"

a BLACKROOM EXPERIENCE night... This time, I made the first move. I asked,

Me: JaLisa what's wrong, you seem a little quiet tonight? How was school today? [*Her reply, simple and curt*]

JaLisa: It was school. (*Sidebar: That is the most irritating response* a child *can give*). I continued my probe asking,

Me: Well if school was just school today, why are you acting different?
(*with a whinny irritated pitch as if wanting me to persist*)

JaLisa: I'm not acting different, Moooooom, there's just nothing to talk about.

Me: Ok, if you say so. Well, are you still friends with that girl who got you in trouble, what was her name?

JaLisa: In trouble when Mom. Which girl?

Me: The one who you gave the answers to in French class, yeah, that one! **JaLisa:** Mom, will you ever let that go?

Me: Yes, but since you seem to have forgotten her name I hope you haven't forgotten that it cost you as well as caused you a lot of trouble. And I am afraid that if you can so easily forget the girl, it will be easy to forget the price you paid. My concern is that you remember so that you never repeat that action.

JaLisa: Mom, you are NOT going to let me forget it, I know. No matter how many times I apologize for cheating in school, you will not trust me again. I have learned my lesson. I will not be that stupid again.

"DID YOU TELL YOUR DAD?" "OR SHOULD I TELL HIM?"

By this time the lights were down low, we had finished cleaning up, and had migrated into the family room, on the couch. Not quite the "BLACKROOM", yet we were having the "experience". These Moments are what this book is all about.

As the conversation continued, Gi's guard went down to me "not trusting" her and a genuine conversation/experience began. This night we sat and laid on the couch in the dark, because our usual spot (my bedroom) was occupied.

This conversation made a few twists and turns, spiraling upward on the topic of trust. Then, she popped the question of the night.

JaLisa: Mom can I trust you?

Me: Of course! (*in my how dare you ask me that voice*) Why would you ask me that?

JaLisa: Do you tell Dad everything I tell you or every time I do something wrong?

    I had to pause, ponder then reply, all in a matter of 2 seconds. If I had taken longer she would have come to her own resolution as an answer to her question. What was I supposed to tell her? If I said, no I do not tell him everything, would I be lying to her? If I said yes, I do, because he is your father and my husband, it is my responsibility to tell him, would that answer cause her to digress in opening up to me during our BLACKROOM EXPERIENCES? This was a turning point and the pendulum was swinging. Time is running out Lisa, answer her!

Me: Huh? What do you mean, do I tell him everything? (*wiping my forehead, relieved that something came out*)

"DID YOU TELL YOUR DAD?" "OR SHOULD I TELL HIM?"

JaLisa: Mom, you know what I mean. Do you tell him about the things we talk about in the dark?

Me: Do you want me to tell him what we talk about?

JaLisa: Mom, I mean, if I wanted him to know, we could just talk in front of him.

Well, this girl is becoming sharp with the answers. It is time that I step up my game and sharpen my answers with a little more preparation prior to questioning her.

This is where I leave my BLACKROOM and ask the question, "Should I tell him what we have talked about privately? Should I force JaLisa to tell him or should I invite him in on our conversations so that he will not feel excluded?" I was quite pinned on the retort to these questions for some time. My desire is that you will perceive or gather the answers as you continue reading-without judgement, stereotype, or accusation-maybe realizing as I did that withholding parental information from a spouse in protection of your child could create unnecessary contention that affects the entire family. The chapter title and event I have chosen to share is very delicate both privately and publicly. Your family dynamics and cultural disciplinary practices may differ. Therefore, remaining focused on the title versus our method of resolution is imperative.

For about 25 years I have trained adults on how to be a mentor to youth. The training manual included topics such as Effective Communications and Characteristics of Youth. These were two topics that always needed to be "tweaked" based on the age, culture, and gender of the mentee. As time passed and many trainings later, we discovered that training the adult mentors exclusively without training the mentees was ineffective. This new relationship was aimed at building an additional life support system for the youth; they too needed to be properly prepared. Therefore, I had to

"DID YOU TELL YOUR DAD?" "OR SHOULD I TELL HIM?"

undertake further research on best practice models for instructing youth at how to value, as well as build, healthy relationships. This process proved to be considerably more advantageous. It has also produced benefits for me in my personal life. Over all my years of research and training, I was oblivious that I was preparing myself for relationship-building as a parent.

What I was learning to share with others assisted me in how to recognize the dynamics in character change in my daughter. Still, despite all my foreknowledge on youth, the way they communicate, behave, act out or respond to adults, I failed to notice a few key communication or character transitions. My daughter, in her own way, was silently yearning for information, awareness and direction. The best way I can describe it is: somehow I remained trapped in a skit being played out in my head as a misinformed, unaware parent who was gravely lacking expertise in non-verbal communication. Oh, how I desired the curtain to drop in my life while I exited stage left, leaving all the props in their place waiting for someone more prepared than I to fulfill the role. Yet, that was not an option. With or without what I deemed as adequate preparation, another BIG "mother crisis" occurred. And I thought I had overcome all the "biggies".

It was JaLisa's 12^h birthday. This is quite honestly when the cell phone saga began. At this early age, I decided that she needed a phone of her own. She was responsible, doing well in school and I wanted to be able to reach her at my leisure while I was working. It has been the culprit, her "partner in crime" ever since. I had all kinds of rules attached to this cell phone. She could not have it turned on while in school. It had to be turned into my room, on my nightstand by 8:00pm on school nights. She could keep it on and with her from Friday after school until Sunday evening at 6:00pm. These were the rules! I just knew that I had put all things in place to secure no glitches in the plan. According to me, I was raising her level of responsibility, training her to be disciplined and accountable with a tool that I was giving her for my leisure. Not saying that she was not elated that I would have such a leisurely need. My need for convenience seemed to often work out to her advantage. It did not seem like that then, but as I am recalling many of our experiences, she tended to be the winner in most if had anything to do with my convenience. First of all, when we as parents make rules for our children, we do not take into account that for those rules to work we have to monitor, manage, HECK! even alter our own lives.

Well, all of my phone rules for JaLisa went great the first two weeks. Subsequently and continuously the success of the "phone rule" dwindled from great to just good. Moreover, after about a year or so, the rule had declined down to me verbalizing a new resolve, "I am not going to pay a phone bill and monitor you. By now you should be responsible without me having to follow up to make sure you are obeying my rules…" Currently, I am writing this thinking, "oh boy, I sure did turn that around to relieve myself of any accountability."

Eventually, by the time JaLisa had turned 14 years old, the rules were still in play, but she had come to be really skilled at knowing my defaults in the area of accountability. I would look at the clock and notice that it was 9:30pm on Wednesday, yet there was no phone on the table. Another time I would notice that I had forgotten to obtain the phone back on Sunday evening, but it was 8:00am Monday (shaking my head at myself). These "hiccups" in my rules continued. Until one day (*which I had once again forgotten to check my nightstand*), as to not default again with accountability, as soon as I remembered I took immediate action. I got up out of my bed, went to JaLisa's bedroom as if to briefly talk and say goodnight. All of the sudden, after neglecting my initial purpose in going to her bedroom, I turned to leave when something clicked in my head (I want to say God told me, but it could have simply been my "mother wit" maturing, becoming more keen). I turned around slowly, bent down low creeping back to her room. She had no clue I was returning, let alone already present in the room, when I noticed a light under her covers. I stilled myself for a Moment and then yelled, "JALISA, ARE YOU ON YOUR CELL PHONE?" Totally in shock to know of my presence she responded "NO MAME!"-I suppose hanging up on whoever she was talking to, quickly. It was a flip phone, so the light went out as soon as the top was shut. I screamed, "WHERE IS YOUR PHONE?" she replied, "I don't know, I forgot to put it in your room." This denial of hers went on for about three minutes, until I felt myself about to boil over. I turned the lights on, finding the thrown phone and I left the room. Well, before I had returned to my room, (which was not far) I speedily contemplated the question, "Could this have been prevented?" Knowing I would have to tell her father of the incident, for surely he heard my amplified voice, I needed a Moment to quickly determine my next move. What if my rules were broken due to my lack of follow-thru, that would not be a good look for me? How far did I really want this to go? Cognizant that once her father saw that I was upset he would immediately assume that he needed to intervene. Like a time clock in my head loudly clicking down; 10, 9, 8, 7, 6, 5, 4, 3, 2, 1, Ding! I was at my bedroom door. I had settled it all in my head and decided that I would not tell him about this one.

Here comes a BIG crisis! About a week later the very same incident happened again, but this time she started this new "LYING" to me thing about the phone. I think she was simply catching on to the fact that my rules were way too much for even me to maintain. For months, it was like a Ping-Pong game; back and forth I would forget to check and she would capitalize on my forgetfulness. Finally, one day I caught her on the phone after 10:00pm. I was over it and her! I had not considered how her having a cell phone was a huge convenience for me. I called her Dad into her room and told him what had happened (without saying how

"DID YOU TELL YOUR DAD?" "OR SHOULD I TELL HIM?"

often…). He was livid!!! He asked her why was she lying about the phone, and that she must be talking to someone she is not supposed to be or there would be no reason for the fabricated story. He took the phone and began to dial resent numbers listed in the phone. He didn't't have to go too far before he figured it out. The VOLCANO erupted!! He gets a young man on the phone who thought my husband was JaLisa calling him back… After they both figured out who it was on the other end of the phone, my husband began to "snap" (talking loud, almost yelling, pissed!!) asking questions like, "How old are you? Do you know how old my daughter is and that she is not allowed to talk to you or any other man? (Ok, the young man may have been 17 years old, was the son of a friend, someone we had known). While he was on the phone (investigating), I was interrogating JaLisa, preparing to obey the scripture in the Bible that says, "Whoever spares the rod hates their children, but the one who loves their children is careful to discipline them". (*NIV Proverbs*

13:24) You either know or can imagine where it went from here...

The next morning, after the house had come to a somewhat calm state, JaLisa woke up for school; eyes swollen from crying and a few marks from her trying to avoid the discipline of the rod... She went to school and I suppose her disposition was a little somber. I was told, her friends inquired, asking her what was wrong, why was she so sad. Then, it just so happened that this would be the semester for swimming. She had to participate. After putting on her swim clothes she returns to the group by the pool. Still a little wimpy, her demeanor provoked more questions, especially with the few welts on her legs from the "rod". Thus, the crisis began. Let me add that JaLisa had always attended a non-diverse school system. Her friends had not been raised as I had been or JaLisa was being raised, as it relates to discipline. Have you noticed I am being as Politically Correct as possible? When her friends saw the fresh welts on her legs, she started

"DID YOU TELL YOUR DAD?" "OR SHOULD I TELL HIM?"

crying and sharing with them what had happened the night before. (*I want to clarify this form of discipline was not regular or abusive*.) Now, as a parent who thought she communicated very well with her child, I was quite shocked that she would go to school sharing this uncommon drama of our house to her friends. Had she forgotten that just a few weeks prior she and this same group of friends went to the Principal's office to express that they felt as if one of their other friends was being abused. Yes, this was BIG, bigger than she could conceptualize. This same group of friends made another trip back to the office "to help" another one of their friends in need. From that point on, it was a nightmare! The school office called in the guidance counselors, who called in the school psychiatrist, who called in Children & Youth Services (CYS). I am presently inhaling very deeply and slowly exhaling. Just the thought of this event sends me to an unhealthy mental zone. Shortly after this event CYS telephoned my mother (because of our constant travel she had guardianship of my children), requesting to meet with her, my husband and myself, at my mother's house. Somehow they had received the story very differently from the Counselor at JaLisa's school. Their presumption was that my husband (a good-sized African-American man) had taken a waist belt to JaLisa and beat her to the point of light bruising (we both bruise easily). Yet, as you read prior, I was the disciplinarian in this entire episode. Their accusations of how the story transpired was radically false. Instantly I came to understand that what the system deemed as "abusive" discipline, was NOT defined the same as my experience as a child, or my culture. In my culture, it is not considered abuse when a child is reprimanded after disobeying a parental rule or instruction, especially if it could ultimately cause them harm or place them in harm's way. When a child knowingly commits negative behaviors, whether chastised by their mother, father, or any trusted, "approved" loved one, we call it discipline. This ideology is supported by the phrase,

"DID YOU TELL YOUR DAD?" "OR SHOULD I TELL HIM?"

"It takes a village to raise a child"-a Nigerian proverb that appears in many different forms in African languages. Its central meaning is that bringing up a child may require an entire community to be connected and engaged in a child's positive development.

Lots of these stories I am sharing are still hard to talk about. At the time that they happened it appeared that we would never see the light of happiness and peace in our home. Thank God, today I can look back in gratitude that I did not give up, or throw in the towel.

I did title this chapter, but am curious as to what would have been your title? _____. Many times youth are influenced by others, by experiences, or by their desires. What would you identify as an "influence" to youth in building healthy relationships with a parent? _____, _____, _____, _____.

BECAUSE THIS IS A SELF HELP BOOK, I AM NOT TELLING YOU TO DISCIPLINE YOUR

CHILD PER MY STORIES. THIS STORY WAS NOT A HAPPY ONE FOR US, WHICH IS ONE OF THE REASONS WHY I AM SHARING. I AM NOT PROMOTING THAT YOU HANDLE YOUR EXPERIENCES IN THIS OR ANY PARTICULAR WAY.

Can you bring to remembrance an incident that occurred during your adult years wherein your anger provoked you to conceal the discussion of an incident that caused an estranged relationship?

THE BLACKROOM EXPERIENCE always brought JaLisa and me back to a place of "building". For example, although a place built with brick may have encountered a vehicle crashing into it, the loosening or even loss of a brick does not necessarily require demolition. It may simply need to be repaired or replaced. In summary, whatever the relationship, if built on the bricks of truth and trust, there is hope. Flawed, but not seamless!

CHAPTER 9
"Is He Mad Or Feeling Excluded?"

Have you ever walked into a room of people talking, but when you enter, straightway their discourse comes to a screeching halt and you awkwardly become the focus of their words? This must have been how my husband felt whenever he would walk in on JaLisa and I having a BLACKROOM Experience. I can recall specific Moments when he would come in the room while we were talking. JaLisa would get quiet, and the comments went like this.

Me: "Hey Honey?"

Him: "Hey, why are you all in the dark, is something wrong?"

Me: "No, we were just talking."

Him: "With the lights out?"

Me: "Yes Honey, you can turn them on, we are finished."

Him: "Never mind, I will go back downstairs."

Most times JaLisa would ask that I not tell her Dad what we were talking about, I think she felt that he was "old fashioned", not open to children sharing in conversation with adults, even in a respectful way. He and I had often discussed how our parents were not at all similar in transparency like today's 21st Century parents. I knew through experience how he felt concerning my transparency with JaLisa. He voiced

"IS HE MAD OR FEELING EXCLUDED?"

frequently that I divulged more than appropriate testimony of my life as a young adult to her.

Although he may have had feelings of exclusion, I was confident that ten minutes in the BLACKROOM would have sent him flipping like a fish out of water, gasping for air. JaLisa was legitimate in feeling suppressed in expressing to her father the majority of issues we addressed in the BLACKROOM. I believe, based on the discussions he and I had previously, she would have gone backwards to the introvert she had left behind.

Occasionally, I wished she felt that I too was "old fashioned". The pressure to listen without reacting may have been minimized. Those were the tough times, when she would ask the tough life questions, and I had absolutely no "on the spot" answers for her adventitious quest. The designless formation of her conversations periodically resulted in the perception that I too was excluded from the talk, even while lying next to her. There were times when I wished my husband would have asked me extended, probing questions pertaining to the conversations in the BLACKROOM. He could have posed the questions similar to a game, questions that were closed ended, leaving me only the uninvolved answers of yes or no.

As fanciful as it sounds, there were many times I envisioned him standing outside of the door holding an empty glass, the open end against the wall with his ear smashed against the closed end. As is his custom, Jimmy likes to know what is going on at all times, everywhere, with everyone. And, even if while she and I were talking, the glass-outside the door route was not taken by him, he would surely inquire at a later time with this predictable inquest, "Why were you and JaLisa talking in the room today, what is going on, is something wrong?" This he asked without fail. If I repeated the same answer as I had previously, often while in the presence of JaLisa, he would get a little perturbed. So, for the sake of parental peace, I shuffled it up a bit. I would respond, "I was just trying to

"IS HE MAD OR FEELING EXCLUDED?"

get JaLisa to communicate her thoughts on the various changes taking place right now in her life, mixed with a little girl talk. Nothing you would want to hear. You know she has to be coerced into sharing, right?" He would acquiesce most times in the beginning of our BLACKROOM EXPERIENCES. But, eventually he stopped accepting my vague words as truth. He began to make statements like, "I hope you are not keeping secrets from me about the kids?" In retrospect, I am not sure if my replies to him were "little lies", or my great mother loyalty to JaLisa. What do you think?

Is it possible that my endeavors to build open, healthy communications with my daughter, cost me my open, healthy communication with my husband? How was I going to keep the peace with Jimmy, while maintaining confidentiality with JaLisa? This was an enormous dilemma for which I had no resolution.

However, no more questions. It was time to pinpoint the answers. This dilemma was one that would affect our entire family, and maybe others. I had to search carefully and thoroughly into every area of our marriage rummaging for the answers. I was confident that my intent was not to lie to my husband or to withhold parental information of which he should be aware. I wanted both my relationship with my husband and my relationship with my daughter to be built on a solid foundation, grow healthy and be able to withstand all and any negative forces against us. I wanted my family!

The quest began with activities in which he and I were regularly involved. I started with our role in our church. For about five years Jimmy and I were Servant-Leaders of Marriage Enrichment, a ministry for married couples at our church. Each month he would plan a gathering for the couples, some were casual fun times together while others were engulfed with deep, intrusive, confronting topics. No one was ever bodacious enough to take ownership of these topics. Nonetheless, rooted beneath the shallow verbal expressions throughout the dialogue lay personal,

"IS HE MAD OR FEELING EXCLUDED?"

"pillow talk" concerns of the couples, that had yet to be resolved in the privacy of their home. These gatherings often turned out to be an opportunity to indirectly address your spouse with matters too sensitive to engage in one-on-one. Having multiple individuals, with diversified views made it a temporary "safe zone" to virtually hash out sensitive subjects.

I can vividly remember our "sensitive subject" time in a Marriage Enrichment gathering. Jimmy was facilitating the discussion and he asked the men, "What is something that your wife does that totally ignites you in a negative way, but you do not bring it up because you know that it is a sensitive issue for her. Maybe it is something that she brought into your marriage as a result of how she was raised…?" The look displayed on my face while he was forming the questions said, "Are you really going to try this here? Do you think I will not attack back like a lioness protecting her cubs? Where are you going with this question?" However, it was only in my facial expression because the question was not directed to the wives, clearly for obvious reason. Slowly, I heard the turning and repositioning of chairs as well as bodies. Each wife situating herself in the direct view of her husband and each husband looking straight-faced glaring at Jimmy. I can only imagine their thoughts towards his setting them up for the kill. Are not men the hunters and we the prey? Not this day. No man uttered a word. They just stared, still like a deer in head lights. Finally, Jimmy said "Come on men, do not be afraid; your wife will appreciate your honesty. We are just sharing our differences in upbringing." Still, not a word. Jimmy then decided that he would be the courageous lion and begin with himself. My initial thought, "Proceed cautiously Mr. Vaughn, this could get ugly." He started off by disclosing the difference in our ages, then to how we were raised very differently. My parents being together my entire life, being Pastors and the number of siblings I have. Next, he explained that all of this was different than how he was raised. He was raised primarily

"IS HE MAD OR FEELING EXCLUDED?"

by his mother. He is the oldest child and the only son. Without exposing the gory details of an exclusive discussion, he ended his expressions with how he felt we are different as it related to prioritizing our quality time together versus the time we spend with our children. I expect you are wondering now just as I was then, "What does this have to do with ANYTHING?" The original question concerned how couples bring individual behaviors into their marriage that do not provoke an attitude of compromising, leaving one of individuals very upset, resulting in unexpressed anger. I, along with several other wives, could not resist the servitude of silence. Eventually, with a sound like cackling hens, flapping our wings while swiftly circling the contained space of a pen we shouted aloud, our disagreement of the shifting point. This went on for several minutes, until Jimmy "cried Uncle", retrieving, and restating his original question. The room regained its solitude. I raised my hand, as if a child in school. Directed towards Jimmy, I asked if I could please ask just one question. He answered "Yes", I said, "It sounds to me that buried in your question is an issue you have yet to express; is that true?" He replied, "Somewhat, but for the sake of discussion I tried to broaden the options to the answers so that none of us would leave here unclear." I thought, without voicing, bad choice, bad discussion and a bad ending. Staring at him, without expression, I said nothing. The group pitched in, creating a more agreeable question, aimed in the path of his point. The night ended with clarity, laughter and always a group hug. I smiled, assisted in the clean-up and headed towards the car. Unfortunate for me this night we were driving in the same vehicle. I silently rode in the passenger seat, patiently waiting for him to ask what was wrong. He did not ask the entire way. Your guess is correct, why ask when he knew the answer. The ride seemed forever, a typical fifteen minutes felt like forty-five minutes.

After we had arrived home, and were in bed, he calmly asked, "Why are you acting funny, being quiet?

Are you upset about something?" My first thought was to sputter a dragon-fire mouth full of "How dare you?" at him all at once, freeing me from the suppression I felt the entire evening. On the contrary, I calmly replied, "Do you have a problem with the time I spend with JaLisa separate from you?" Conscious of the fact that he was totally shocked by my reply, I waited. In due time, he said, "I do not have a problem with you spending time with JaLisa, but I do think you should spend more time ensuring that our relationship is growing healthy, because if we are ok than JaLisa will be ok." Pleasantly surprised at his forwardness, I listened, pondered then said, "Ok".

I concluded with the "ok", because whether I agreed or disagreed I understood the intent of his heart.

THE BLACKROOM EXPERIENCE was an intentional time set aside for JaLisa and me to express, build and grow a healthy relationship. I was extremely intentional at being present and accounted for whenever she needed. My husband had noticed my intentionality with that relationship, not desiring anything less for JaLisa and me. Nevertheless, he had also noticed that I did not pursue the same intentionality in our marriage relationship. It was crystal clear that I needed a balance. Not knowing where to begin, I asked him what could I do for him in order that he be confident in knowing how important both my marriage and my parenting were to me. Without ever presuming to define a perfect path to the answer, I know this one thing of a certainty: every relationship needs the same ingredients for health and growth and that is 20% sunshine, 20% rain, 20% listening, 20% talking, 20% shade (personal space) and still 100% intentionality, always. I have learned that Jimmy was neither mad or feeling excluded, but rather he, or should I say we, must remain intentional at our own "together-time". A Darkroom is preferred, (wink, wink). A place where we can produce and develop as Godly examples to our children.

CHAPTER 10

"Life after the BLACKROOM"

As I lie here in the dark thinking of all the things we've been through, I am amazed that we made it to her 21st birthday. I would have thought that by now things would be much different. I would have also assumed that my parenting requirements and roles would be different. Even now, I am coming to realize that with time and maturity I am needed to a greater degree now than I was when JaLisa was an infant. The need is solicited in a much different fashion. She no longer solely needs my instructions, my opinions or even my experiences. She needs me to be a Parental-Mentor. That is, me mostly sharing my life experiences with her as a navigation tool for her on the way to her new experiences that she is presently embarking upon, versus me instructing her on what she must do. She needs me to be a Parental-Coach. I am aware that my opinion is valued differently by her. Now, I provide her with encouragement as she makes decisions, whether I agree or disagree. I counsel her on the multitude of options provided to her, in order that she is willing to live with those choices she makes. Hence, I challenge her to choose wisely, because her decisions determine her destiny. So, "Make it count!" I am now someone who is willing to listen to her at all times, especially in the light, while not feeling shame, fear or of regret about how my response will be received or interpreted by her. I am no longer teaching her how to physically walk, I am walking with her both physically as well as spiritually and providing sheer guidance as we stroll through the geography of life. Our strides are wide, ambitious and continuous. We are on her path that God has laid before her. I gladly take a back seat, living in total agreement with His process for the rest of her life.

As I write today, it is JaLisa's 22nd birthday. I lie in dark, once again thinking about her, our times and our conversations. I am thinking about the many, many BLACKROOM EXPERIENCEs. I find myself missing her more than ever. But her life is changed as well as mine.

Life moves along. Now she has graduated from college and living in the state where she has accepted employment. Wow, that would officially make her a grown woman. We are in two different physical locations, but our hearts are still entwined. At this point in our lives, my once attached umbilical cord, although severed, has relocated to our hearts, creating a permanent bond stronger than any three-stranded rope.

Reminiscing about her last semester in college, JaLisa and I talked on the phone at least four times a day. However, the first three years were not at all like the last semester. I have been trying to mark the day, date and time when things changed. It all remains inconclusive.

Once JaLisa was accepted to Syracuse University (SU), she created a Facebook page specifically for girls who were entering their Freshman year at the school. Maybe this was the beginning of the change. She apparently desired to meet others outside of our "camp". The process of separation had begun. She was using skills that would soon be perfected, resulting in a life career. I refused to omit these as meager Moments. Seeking out those most like her; uncertain of the upcoming terrain, she asked them questions. Questions like; "Why did you select SU? Do any of you attend church? What will be your major? Was anyone accepted in the iSchool?" I am sure the questioning went beyond this, but along these lines. This private group on social media is where she met her first roommate. JaLisa maintained this group that swiftly flourished in numbers. By the time the first semester began, there were more than 500 girls who

"LIFE AFTER THE BLACKROOM"

had joined the private group. She continued this group up to her Junior year, with more than 2,000 girls as friends, increasing daily.

The first semester of her first year in college, our relationship took on new shape, not drastic, just new. Much like changing from a square to a rectangle. She called multiple times per day, once in the morning, always before an exam (we prayed prior to her going in the class room) and at night. Then, she met a group of girlfriends. She became connected to them so quickly that I questioned the genuineness of the relationships.

First, it was her freshman year roommate, who I call Missy. She was from a totally different world than JaLisa had ever experienced. Missy is Dominican, her primary language is Spanish, she is very outspoken, and outgoing. None of these key elements of Missy's persona merged with JaLisa. Therefore, JaLisa had to learn how to be strong in character and confident in her convictions or she would be swallowed up whole in the dorm room before facing the entire campus population. There were struggles initially, but they learned a secret, we can "agree to disagree". I was shocked, JaLisa took on a totally new strength. In the beginning of her adjustment she would call, complaining to me about EVERYTHING her roommate had done that was not like what she had experienced or had been taught. Suddenly, she wanted to move off-campus, get a new roommate, and the list goes on... All of which I emphatically answered with "No". I said "JaLisa college is all about you learning how to live in the world with people who are not like you. Yet, it is an opportunity for you to begin to be an entirely different person." I told her, she should make up a nickname for herself and when asked your name, give them the name you always wanted to be called by, like "Tootsie". She thought I was being ridiculous, but I was serious. I encouraged her to take on a stronger, bolder, character so that people would not take advantage of her or overstep her boundaries. As mentioned in the beginning chapters of this book, I have remained somewhat an extremist. My point was that she would take on this enormous, mean, cold, exciting world with a new perspective. No one knew who she was prior. No one knew what she liked to eat or that she never had a boyfriend. I am not promoting a life of lies, rather a life full of expansion of horizons and branching out on limbs. There is no error in branching outside of your comfort zone. I saw this as launching towards positive discovery of herself, in contrast to taking the old her into a new world. Why lay when you can launch? The launching pad was made active as soon as she moved into her dorm room, with a person whom she had never laid eyes upon. The end result from my perspective was that she listened to a minuscule portion of what I recommended. My view from Pennsylvania, via the telephone, was that she was forced out of all places of comfort and rocketed into outer spaces that I renamed as the following: Me'ers vs. Mars, JaLisater vs. Jupiter, Vices vs. Venus, Meditation vs. Mercury, Negativism vs.

Neptune, Unity vs. Uranus, Self-esteem vs. Saturn, and finally Evolution on Earth. By this time, she had evolved into a young lady who was over the "it is all about ME", to knowing the JaLisa without the daily direction, expectation or definition of parents, grandparents or church people making life for her what we wanted it to be. The EVOLUTION of JaLisa Eugenia-Chaye Vaughn was erupting on earth. This young lady had found out that she was not perfect, there were a few vices, some good and some not so good. This JaLisa was understanding the personal value of meditation; personal time in prayer. She ceased from identifying the negativity in others to detecting positivity in both them as well as herself. She entered the unity of thought that I must learn to exist in this environment with others who appear to be extremely different from myself. Diversity was no longer an enemy. These recognitions drastically raised her self-esteem. Once the bar was raised and the imagination of self had been released from the cage of her own mind. She was free to be... Evolution was inevitable.

Somewhere in the evolution JaLisa had a lapse of memory thinking that she was in control of her life. She forgot that not having to answer to her parents was simply a slice of the pie not the entire pie. There was still God, the same God she had accepted into her life (not by force) as Lord and Savior. She served Him for years and prayed to, at minimum, every Friday morning 5:00 AM sharp. She lapsed on the memory that for eighteen years, every Sunday morning without fail, she could be found in church singing on the youth choir, worshiping and praising God, in fellowship with like believers. This was not merely tradition this was her life.

I recall the time when JaLisa had called me crying and panting as if someone had done something to her. It was a Sunday afternoon. I had just come in the house from church. I calmly asked her, "What is wrong, why are you crying so hard? Did someone do something to you?" She replied with sniffing and blowing her nose, then some verbiage which I could not decipher came out. I stopped her, asking, "JaLisa did something bad happen?" She composed herself enough to reply, "No Ma'am, no one did anything to me." My response, "Then why are you crying so hard?". She replied, "I do not know, Mom. I was in my room and I turned on the television. A gospel show was on and I just "went in" (for us this means that one submits to God in intense praise). She continued, "I got up out of the bed and started praying. Then I searched on my iPod for all the "shouting" (dancing in the spirit) church music I had. I began to have church right in my room. Mom I need to find a church here, immediately." I chuckled and said, "You are right, that is what you need to do." A huge exhale of relief came out of me. My first response after gaining clarity, now let us pray. Smack dab into prayer I went. I did as she was doing. I "went in"; thanking God for His presence and His power. She was simultaneously thanking God, asking for forgiveness and giving Him glory for the reminder of who He is to her. Later that week, she called her Dad and asked him if he would get in contact with the Pastor he had introduced her to while moving into her dorm.

What happened with JaLisa was she had been away in school for about two months. She was living the life of a Freshman in college to infinity and beyond. Fellowship with God along with church attendance was not the order of her days anymore. Of course, this change of heart brought joy and light to the example that we had been while she was at home.

JaLisa not only started attending the church, she gathered together van loads of students to attend weekly with her. She continued with that congregation until graduating.

To all the parents reading this book, we cannot badger our children into living a Godly life. We can only commit to consistently being examples of every principle and practice that we present to them. Because, when they are away from us they remember more of what we have been examples of, than what we have demanded of them. I had to repent to God and occasionally to JaLisa for the inconsistent example I sometimes displayed. During those times, I was also misrepresenting God. We must regularly take full responsibility for our actions remembering that we are accountable to not only God but also to our children.

Thankfully, JaLisa and Missy were surviving their freshman year of college. The two of them were soon introduced to the next group of friends, Ale and Tel. Speedily a friendship tie was knotted. They stuck together like magnets, learning each day how to cultivate life-long friendships. It was evident that Jalisa had enjoyed personal growth in her first year of college, including the physical growth. The term "freshman 15" was more like "freshman 20". Every time she came home to visit people were commenting on her weight gain. "Freshman 15" is a phrase adopted for college freshman, primarily girls who had gained at least 15 pounds from eating differently while adjusting to being away from home. Determined to not be defeated concerning this topic, as I was early in her life, I carefully and confidently told her, "No worries daughter, stop weighing yourself for a while, college is stressful. Feel free to ignore anyone who references your weight, forever!"

Another taxing issue for JaLisa while away from home was "Who is going to do my hair?" I still fail to understand how that became a priority while pursuing a higher education. When I was in college we wore ponytails, and sweat pants. I was clear that full adaptation to college life had not taken place. She searched and researched online trying to find someone on or off-campus who sold quality hair weave. She required someone who was accomplished at sewing in weave. At home, we frequently called JaLisa a Weavologist. Back then she knew more about weaved hair than her major in school. A last, she received a response from a then quiet, student. When she met this girl, you would have thought JaLisa had hit the lottery! Her excitement was as one who finally picked that winning lotto number, enabling her to wholly satisfy a 4-year college tuition at this private institution. On the contrary, she had merely satisfied her personal need for a private beautician while at school. This friend merged into the pack of friends as smoothly as freshly melted butter. They were the "Fierce and Fabulous Five". They went everywhere together during the semester. They even planned their first Summer traveling state-to-state visiting one another. This pack had the appearance of life-long friendship. I, along with the other mothers was being replaced right before my eyes.

Entering the Sophomore year was less ruffled, more tranquil. Nonetheless it would hold its own challenges. JaLisa was about to turn 20 years old. No more teenager. I almost lost recognition of her due to social media. The daughter that I had raised to be classy, God-fearing, discreet and reserved, was posting pictures revealing more of everything! The total opposite of what I had taught her. This was the semester in which she had her first "real boyfriend", real meaning, she changed her Facebook status to "In a relationship". This was significant in the world of social media. What was the world coming to? I admit I was actually happy that she was allowing herself to trust on another level. I wanted to know, even at 20 years old, how she would handle a romantic relationship. It was about time. JaLisa was all in with this relationship. What I felt about her dress attire, late nights and academic success, was no concern of hers. She had made friends and now a boyfriend. The phrase she was "smelling herself" did not compare to the aroma she was secreting. I was displeased, but her father had a significantly worse distain for her behavior. It seemed like he and I were having daily arguments of how I should "make her" remove her post. To him, she did not have on enough clothes, she was too close to guys (or they were touching her inappropriately) and she had a glass in her hand (which to him, meant she was drinking alcohol). The complaint scroll continued. I asked myself, "Why was this only my problem? Why was I the blame for her explorations as well as exploitations? Why would he not speak to her himself? These were all his complaints. I do not recommend you to try to answer any of them. They were specific to our situation. However, it would not hurt if you attempted to tailor questions that fit the perimeters of your experiences, especially if you have or have had young adult children. I am sure you probably have your very own conclusion to this saga. For the sake of peace in my home, none of these questions did I speak out of my mouth. Yet, they were creating traffic jams in my head. I had to find a way to get through to JaLisa without completely losing her. She was not in reach to physically force her to change her clothing or create a wedge between her and her boyfriend. I wanted her to know that I was disappointed with her decisions without disconnecting her; potentially forfeiting years of relationship building. I wanted her to explore without exploiting herself. Simply put, I wanted to go to SU and have a sit down with her, despite my feelings that this situation had far exceeded the level of success that a sit-down conversation had produced early on. That would not work at this juncture. My one and only resolution was that this degree of desperation required that I pray earnestly for my daughter, not the same mundane prayers that I had prayed when she was in the house, down the hall, in her bedroom. This situation was affecting my family, my marriage, even my son. It demanded that my prayers be power-packed, fueled to travel over the miles, from Pittsburgh to Syracuse faster than the speed of light. I desired God to do in five seconds what I was uncertain five hours of travel would accomplish. I prayed and I prayed and I prayed. I prayed for hours, I prayed for days. I continued to converse over the phone with JaLisa, as if all was well. Immediately after my finger pressed the end call button on the phone, I dropped to my knees, crying out to God.

I PRAYED!

God have mercy on my child, speak to her, love on her, convict her and cover her with Your blood. I am pleading on her behalf for Your protection; send your angels on assignment, keeping her from dangers seen and unseen. I pray that You would shield her from herself. God please hear my heart's cry for my child. You know my heart and you know hers as well. I need you to let her know that you are with her, that you see her, and that you are concerned about everything that concerns her. I ask that you not allow her to be abused, bullied, or submit to the enticement of the enemy. You have kept and preserved her to this day. I am confident that you have a divine plan and purpose for her life, one that she cannot perceive. Arrest her spirit, rapture her in your loving arms. I thank you God for lending her to me and teaching me how to train her in your ways. You said in your word, "Train up a child in the way that he/she should go, and when he/she is old he/she will not depart from it." (Proverbs 22:6). Father I give you back your word, I stand on your word and I believe your word. I have done all that I know to do to train up JaLisa. Now God, she is in your hands. I ask that you give Jimmy and me your peace in the process that you have designed for her. I ask that you help us to stay out of your way as you mold her, make her and finish the fulfillment of your plan in her life. I thank you in advance for the completed work, full manifestation of your will. Thank you for being God in JaLisa's life! Thank you for showing her how great and mighty you are on her journey to maturity. Thank you for faith to believe! Thank you for faith to release her to you! I seal this prayer with the confession that you are King of Kings and Lord of Lords, there is NO-THING too hard for you.

In Jesus name I pray, AMEN!

It was 5 minutes after this praying this prayer that I felt the peace of God in me, in my husband, in my house and even in JaLisa. She started asking me "Mom can you look at these pictures and tell me which one I should post?" THANK YOU JESUS!! That bullet was dodged. No, she did not always agree or post my selection, that was not my focus. Yes, there were times that we had disagreements, but they did not divide us. I knew God was at work and His angels were on assignment. I only had the task of trusting Him by continuing in steadfast, unmovable prayer. My faith in God was no longer shaken when she did things of which I disagreed.

The Sophomore semester ended successfully. The "Fierce-Fabulous Five" remained connected through a multiplicity of phone calls to parents, me praying with them on the phone as they traveled for Spring breaks, or when they were about to take exams about topics they were anxious or unprepared to test on. I prayed for those girls as I prayed for JaLisa. I realized that they had become a package. If JaLisa was going to be in a sister/friend relationship with them, the same Jesus that had a purpose for JaLisa's life, must also have a purpose for their lives.

JaLisa was relishing in her college life so much that she asked if she could take Summer classes to ensure an on-time graduation. We agreed. Straightway, I knew there was additional reasoning as to why year-round school instantaneously became appealing. She adamantly proclaimed the single purpose was academically based, along with the fact that she did not want to work a job all Summer. Sounds good, right? Her Dad agreed. She had to know that I was aware that her boyfriend, who was a football player, would also be there during these Summer sessions. It is a requirement of the sport. Nevertheless, I too had an unexpressed motive. I did not buck the plan, knowing that there was a seed of anxiousness about the possibility of us disagreeing on her existing curfew. Her two weeks home for break would be just about enough time before a war of ages could began. I had gotten comfortable with our home schedule. My son was requiring his own level of expression with me which I titled "stool talk". This occurred every day after school. He was not a night owl, mainly due to his stringent sports, academic and workout demands. I did not want her coming home distracting him with her adult-like hours. Therefore, I gladly went along with her shenanigan of Summer classes.

JaLisa was back home. She had her car so she was able to venture, but she did not have her friends (the Fierce-Fabulous), so she stayed in and slept for five days. I am assuming that the life she was living in Syracuse was a rough one. By the seventh day some "cabin fever" was setting in. Still she refused to embrace any level of entertainment without her friends. Somewhat concerned, I asked why she would not go out and have some fun. Was it because she had no one to hang out with? Her answer was, "No that's not the reason." She said there were lots of people asking her to go out. She simply did not want to go out. Over excited that we had made it through the first week of Summer break, I stopped inquiring.

There was one week left before JaLisa would travel back to SU. There was a girl that had been inviting her out for quite a long time. She said, "Mom, she has been inviting me out for more than a year now. I constantly say no making up excuses as to why. Do you thing I should go?" I respond, "It is totally up to you JaLisa, where does she want to go?" This discussion went back and forth like a pendulum, ceasing to halt. The evening was drawing nigh and no decision. I had had a sufficient serving of her indecisiveness, yelling up the steps I say, "JaLisa this is not Syracuse, you cannot wait until midnight to decide you want to leave the house. Are you going or not?" There were waves of frustration in the amplification of my tone. She begrudgingly answered, "Yes Mom, I am trying to find something to wear." Now comes the discussion I did not desire having with my husband. "Honey, what time did you tell JaLisa to be home"? I asked with much reservation. He replies the norm, with another question, "I don't know Honey, what time did you tell her?" Here we go again, I was thinking. With my eyes rolling up in my head, attempting to react without being a smart-aleck, I paused before saying, "Honey, that is your call not mine. I simply do not want to hear your mouth later." That said, he replies, "I told her 1:00 AM." Fireworks were exploding in my mouth. Restraining from parting my lips, I applied an invisible muzzle, as not to erupt verbally. You see, I have learned, that once I give my husband the reins on a decision, I cannot take them back due to "I disagree with how you are holding and controlling the reins." Yes, the ones I gave him. I have strived long and hard for a strategy in choosing my battles. In the process, I am benefiting from the partnership of good as well as bad parental decision-making. When I am not in control, the weight of the decision is shared. This night was, in the worst way, the best example of this.

Around 8:00 PM JaLisa was ready to leave the house. She tells us where they are going. Jimmy and I decide that due to the location, it would best if she drives to the house of the girl, park the car and ride with her. She agrees and leaves out. 10 minutes later she returns and says, "I can't believe I left my shoes!"; while puffing up the steps to her room. She leaves back out again. She had not quite reached her destination she calls me, expressing how she does not want to go. Yet she was in route. I recommended that she goes, stays for a short period and then leaves. She replies, "Mom how can I leave if my car is at her house?" "That is true, Gi. Well call me if you want to leave before she does and either your Dad or I will come get you." The evening goes by, no pick me up calls. I resolve that things are going better than she thought. It is Saturday night, church the next day as well as Mother's Day. I bring my night to a close and go up to bed. Jimmy and Carrington had already gone ahead of me. It took a while for me to fall asleep, but it did not last long. I turned over and looked at the clock (it was 1:00 AM). I nudge Jimmy to ask "Has JaLisa come in yet?" Probably irritated at my interruption of his sleep he answers, "I do not know, I am asleep. Did you check her room?" I was not willing to take the walk, so I attempted at falling back to sleep. It was less than 10 minutes later; Jimmy's cell phone rang. He jumps straight upright in the bed, startled by the ring.

Jimmy: Hello

JaLisa: Dad someone hit me, the car. Dad, Dad!!! (*Hysterical*)

Jimmy: What? JaLisa? Are you ok? Where are you? (*Yelling in the phone*)

Still startled from the abrupt awakening, he was sounding confused. I was in the background, trying to hear her voice and understand them both. While Jimmy and JaLisa were talking at each other, at the same time, someone took the phone from JaLisa. The voice was that of a stranger, someone neither she nor we knew.

Female Stranger: Hello Sir. Your daughter was in an accident. She appears to be ok. I have called the police. You need to get here quick!

Jimmy: Get where, where is she? Is she is ok?

Female Stranger: I am not sure of the address, it is on Penn Avenue, between Penn and Liberty. Do you know where Arsenal Middle School is? She is on the street at the backside of the school. Sir! Get here quick, the police are checking your daughter and about to take her. I was just walking up the street and saw the accident. (click)

Jimmy dropped the phone, ran to the closet and began dressing. Trying not to awaken or alarm my son, I followed his actions. All while asking questions, endeavor to retrieve any amount of information on what happened, where my daughter is, who was that women and where are we going? He was afraid and nervous. I could see and feel it. Frustrated at my interrogating, he randomly threw out answers that absolutely made no sense. I quieted myself and went into prayer. Loud, then soft, openly and internally. A fear had gripped my soul that only God could release. Everything in me was in a knot. All I could say was JESUS, JESUS, JESUS, JESUS, JESUS!!!!!! We got in the car, he was driving. We pulled out of the driveway, down the street, confusingly we did not know where to go. We tried to call the "Female Stranger" back on the number recorded in his call list, but there was no answer and no voice message. We started calling the relatives of the girl JaLisa went out with and they were of no assistance. Eventual we come close to the street that he thought the stranger said the accident had taken place. Our heartbeats were getting slower yet harder.

Neither of us could breathe. He continued driving, but the speedometer was decreasing in speed. We were not ready for any of this. We arrive on the street of the accident. There is pitch blackness. All that we could see was the glare of broken glass spreading from one pole to the next. Fluid of some sort was running down the street, faucet like. WHERE IS MY DAUGHTER? GOD, WHERE IS MY DAUGHTER?

After 30 minutes of calls to family, friends, hospitals and police stations, finally, someone gave us some guidance. We were sent to a police station on the other side of town. Upon arrival, we asked questions pleading for any indication of the location and condition of our child. They provided no substantial confirmation that we were in the right place or that JaLisa was here, at hospital, or in jail. These were the worst minutes of the worst night of my life. "GOD WHERE ARE YOU? Please send my daughter to us. We need You to bring her to us now, alive, and safe!" This is all I remember praying. We sat a few minutes more when out of a door came a police officer. He asked if we were looking for our daughter? We stand up, like military soldiers answering, "Yes, is she here? Where is she?" Quieting us with hand gesture, he responds, "Yes." We persist, verbally attacking him with all of the unanswered questions of the night. He says, "She is here. She is ok, but I need to brief you on the report and have you sign off." Honestly, we did not care in the least about his report, "Give me my daughter!", I said. Jimmy appropriately reacting, responded, "Sir, can you please just give me the papers to sign so I can see my daughter?" While Jimmy was signing, JaLisa walks out of the door. I grab her away from the person at the door, hug her and we quickly removed ourselves from the dehumanizing premise.

Crying, hugging, examining her, all in a matter of one minute. We get in the car; Jimmy driving, JaLisa in the back seat and I next to her. In a daze, appearing as if she was in shock or drugged. She relentlessly apologized, while saying she did not know what had happened. I settled her and told her to go to sleep. Relieved that she was alive, breathing on her own and not in a hospital or jail, I sought to comfort my husband, checking to see if he had taken a breath as of yet. He simply nodded his head. Speechless by the drama of the past hours. In spite of it all, we had her with us. Her blouse was bloody, but she was not bleeding. She was bruised and glass cut, but not a broken bone. She smelled like a saloon, but able to speak. Two cars were totaled, but her life was saved. THANK YOU GOD!

Pulling into the garage I awakened her, asking; "How do you feel Gi, does anything hurt? Can you walk to your room?" In a soft tone, she answered, "Yes ma'am". I got her to her room. Jimmy went to our room, I checked on Carrington in his room, then back to JaLisa. Sitting on the couch at the end of her bed, I helped her take off her now blood drenched clothes (as the glass continued to surface from her skin, it increased the bleeding) and into bed. I had no words, I just stared at her. My mind was confused. What I was seeing? Was this a similar experience I once had? The scent in the air and what I was feeling were as disconnected as a surgical amputation of a body part. I continued to cry out, "Jesus, please help me with this." This was not manifesting as merely intoxication anymore. Has my daughter been drugged? It was deja vu, I had seen this before. These are the signs of someone slipping a drug in your drink. I had experienced this before. In that Moment, spiritual surgery was being done in me, God was reconnecting the tubes so that I could understand what to do next. At some point, in this seemingly unending distress I called my best friend who prayed for me and spoke words of life into JaLisa that I was not able to do right then. Once again I did what I know to do for the answers needed. I got in the bed with JaLisa, wrapped my entire body around hers and began speaking life into her body. I quoted every scripture in the Bible that I could think of, giving God His word concerning my child. If you have not noticed prayer was becoming a "natural reflex" of mine. Have you ever gone to your doctor for a physical and they pulled out the little hammer like tool to check your reflex? At the contact of the hammer on the correct spot of your kneecap, up springs your lower leg. You neither force it nor aide it, yet it responds automatically to the pressure of the tool applied to a nerve. Reflex is an action performed as a response to a stimulus and without conscious thought. Now, when I pray, it is precisely a natural reflex. I am responding to the stimulus of life that overwhelmed me at that moment. It is not a "plan B", or a second thought. Without conscious thought life's stimulus sent me to my knees, seeking mercy, grace, guidance and instructions. When I began this book, I was not at the place that I have grown to in prayer. Back then I sought answers from others, depending on their approval of my next move. This left me in the dark concerning so many things. My life of prayer has brought me into the light of God's love and power. My parenting is in His control. He is the power source of my light and all life.

Prayer changes EVERYTHING! JaLisa survived the accident physically, yet bruised emotionally. She became another person. I was concerned with her emotional outbreaks. We could all be sitting around laughing and having fun; I would look at JaLisa seconds later and she was staring off into space. She zoned out often and would cry over the simplest of things. I wondered if she had hit her head. She did tell me that she was still removing glass out of skin weeks after the accident. I thought I had the correct process. I took her to the doctor's, the week of the accident and, aside from bruising and minor cuts, it was concluded that she survived an accident that should have killed her. Lord was I grateful! While yet scrutinizing the event, I wondered if she would ever come to herself. The self she was prior to the accident. I was blaming myself, JaLisa and Jimmy. I felt we had all taken part in this horrifying night. I noticed that I was growing more and more angry every day, but at whom and for what? This event remains sensitive to talk about. I am sharing it with the world because it was a turning point in our relationship. I did not have the BLACKROOM as a respite for our aching hearts and divided thoughts. I do not have darkness to cover myself or my daughter's mistakes. Still I was required to be her loving mother; listening, looking and lurking for answers to get her to her next place in life with the help of God. She needed me to be something different in this place. We were in the light and she did not need me reacting as if we had no BLACKROOM EXPERIENCES. Yes, the BLACKROOM was full of light and I was assuming the task of convincing her that even without the BLACKROOM, nothing in this world could take away our experiences. For it is all of our experiences collectively that have ushered us into the light. I was now to be an example of this light to her and her friends, whether we are near or far.

Within a few days of the accident several of JaLisa friends flew into town to check on her. Rakeeta, her assumed blood sister, who lived with us for some time, dropped everything and came from college in Georgia. The minute she landed and laid eyes on JaLisa she said, "JaLisa, there is nothing wrong with you. Why did you have me and Auntie Nita thinking you were half dead? Hug me, I am glad that you are alright, but you really had us scared." This was also the sentiments of two other friends, who as well came to see about their friend.

Once the gang was all in and JaLisa was receiving 24-hour loving care, I had a chance to get alone and make some decisions. How was I going to get her back to school? Since the accident she was trying to reattach the umbilical cord, and she would not leave my side. She spoke of transferring from Syracuse to a local college. ABSOLUTELY NOT, was my thought. I had about three days to rebuild her confidence in driving, prepare her car, and send her to Summer school. Remember that? I knew that with the help of God and her sister/friends she could get behind the wheel to continue the life purposed for her from birth.

"LIFE AFTER THE BLACKROOM"

JaLisa did change extremely from this experience. She matured, becoming more focused on what really mattered. She valued her life as the precious jewel that I worked so intently at getting her to envision. Guess what? It did not come through or happen with the process that I had planned. But, it happened. It was thus far the greatest experience in love and trust of our "Life after the BLACKROOM".

Today JaLisa is a graduate of Syracuse University with a Bachelor of Science Degree in Information Technology. She accomplished being on the Dean's List, and accepted a professional job with a major technology company in Texas. She has started and is managing two successful businesses. As of one month ago, JaLisa is living in her own apartment, which is fully furnished. A self-sufficient beautiful young lady, who loves God and people. She is giving, considerate, and rational. Where did that come from? (Smiling) She serves God and her community, by sharing her testimony of His grace.

You see after all it was not the location of our experiences that made the difference in our lives, but rather the commitment coupled with intentionality of building a relationship full of many experiences plastered anywhere in the world. Only a life of prayer can manifest this level of parental commitment. I challenge you to find a place, commit to a person, be it family, friend or foe, and begin building experiences that travel from **BLACKROOMS** to a world of abundant life and glorious **LIGHT**! Now, flip the switch. **LIGHTS ON!**